TREES
OF
MICHIGAN

IDENTIFICATION
RECORD BOOK

D1559688

Dr. Moss

Your Feedback is Appreciated!!!

Please consider leaving us "5 Stars" on your
Amazon review.

Thank you!

This Tree Identification Record Book
Belongs To:

_____

There are 100's of tree species found in the state of Michigan! With more than 14 billion trees growing in the state, it equates to approximately 20 million acres of forest land - that's over 52% of the entire state being covered in forests. The most common tree species are the balsam fir, red maple and sugar maple.

Use this record book to identify and record the many types of trees you come across!

Environment

Location / GPS: _____ Date _____

Season: ○ Spring   ○ Summer   ○ Fall   ○ Winter

Surroundings: ○ Hedgerows   ○ Field   ○ Park   ○ Woodland   ○ Water
○ Other_____

Setting: ○ Natural   ○ Artificial   Type: ○ Evergreen   ○ Deciduous

Notes: _____
_____

General

Shape: ○ Vase   ○ Columnar   ○ Round   ○ (Other) _____

Features: ○ Conical/Spire   ○ Spreading   ○ Upright   ○ Weeping
○ (Other) _____

Branching: ○ Opposite   ○ Alternate   Estimated Age: _____

Notes: _____
_____

Needles or Leaves

Type: ○ Needle   ○ Simple Broadleaf   ○ Compound Broadleaf   ○ Scales

Shape: ○ Cordate (heart-shaped)   ○ Lanceolate (long and narrow)
○ Deltoid (triangular)   ○ Obicular (round)   ○ Ovate (egg-shaped)
○ Palm and Maple   ○ Lobed

Structure: ○ Simple (attached to twigs or twig stems)
○ Compound (attached to single lead steam)

Notes: _____
_____

Flowers, Fruits & Seeds

Flower Type: ○ Single Blooms   ○ Clustered Blooms   ○ Catkins

Fruits / Seeds: ○ Berries   ○ Apples   ○ Pears   ○ Nuts   ○ Acorns
○ Cones   ○ Capsules   ○ Catkins   ○ (Other) _____

Notes: _____
_____

Leaf Buds & Twigs

Bud Type: ○ Terminal (grows at tip of a shoot causing shoot to grow longer)
○ Lateral (grow along sides of a shoot causing sideways growth)

Twig Features: ○ Smooth   ○ Hairy   ○ Spines   ○ Corky Ribs
○ (Other) _____

Notes: _____

Bark

Texture: ○ Furrowed   ○ Scaly   ○ Peeling   ○ Smooth   ○ Shiny
○ Fissured   ○ Ridges / Depressions   ○ Papery   ○ Warty
○ (Other) _____

Color: ○ Gray   ○ Brown   ○ Cinnamon   ○ White   ○ Silver
○ Green   ○ Copper   ○ (Other) _____

Notes: _____

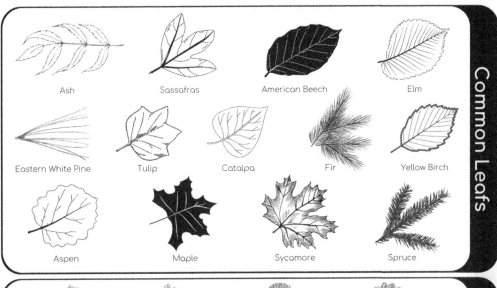

Ash

Sassafras

American Beech

Elm

Eastern White Pine

Tulip

Catalpa

Fir

Yellow Birch

Aspen

Maple

Sycamore

Spruce

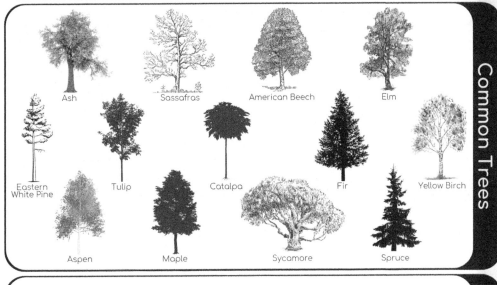

Ash

Sassafras

American Beech

Elm

Eastern White Pine

Tulip

Catalpa

Fir

Yellow Birch

Aspen

Maple

Sycamore

Spruce

Environment

Location / GPS: _____ Date _____

Season: ◯ Spring ◯ Summer ◯ Fall ◯ Winter

Surroundings: ◯ Hedgerows ◯ Field ◯ Park ◯ Woodland ◯ Water
◯ Other _____

Setting: ◯ Natural ◯ Artificial   Type: ◯ Evergreen ◯ Deciduous

Notes: _____
_____

General

Shape: ◯ Vase ◯ Columnar ◯ Round ◯ (Other) _____

Features: ◯ Conical/Spire ◯ Spreading ◯ Upright ◯ Weeping
◯ (Other) _____

Branching: ◯ Opposite ◯ Alternate   Estimated Age: _____

Notes: _____
_____

Needles or Leaves

Type: ◯ Needle ◯ Simple Broadleaf ◯ Compound Broadleaf ◯ Scales

Shape: ◯ Cordate (heart-shaped) ◯ Lanceolate (long and narrow)
◯ Deltoid (triangular) ◯ Obicular (round) ◯ Ovate (egg-shaped)
◯ Palm and Maple ◯ Lobed

Structure: ◯ Simple (attached to twigs or twig stems)
◯ Compound (attached to single lead steam)

Notes: _____
_____

Flowers, Fruits & Seeds

Flower Type: ◯ Single Blooms ◯ Clustered Blooms ◯ Catkins

Fruits / Seeds: ◯ Berries ◯ Apples ◯ Pears ◯ Nuts ◯ Acorns
◯ Cones ◯ Capsules ◯ Catkins ◯ (Other) _____

Notes: _____
_____

Leaf Buds & Twigs

Bud Type: ◯ Terminal (grows at tip of a shoot causing shoot to grow longer)
◯ Lateral (grow along sides of a shoot causing sideways growth)

Twig Features: ◯ Smooth ◯ Hairy ◯ Spines ◯ Corky Ribs
◯ (Other) _____

Notes: _____

Bark

Texture: ◯ Furrowed ◯ Scaly ◯ Peeling ◯ Smooth ◯ Shiny
◯ Fissured ◯ Ridges / Depressions ◯ Papery ◯ Warty
◯ (Other) _____

Color: ◯ Gray ◯ Brown ◯ Cinnamon ◯ White ◯ Silver
◯ Green ◯ Copper ◯ (Other) _____

Notes: _____

Ash

Sassafras

American Beech

Elm

Eastern White Pine

Tulip

Catalpa

Fir

Yellow Birch

Aspen

Maple

Sycamore

Spruce

Ash

Sassafras

American Beech

Elm

Eastern White Pine

Tulip

Catalpa

Fir

Yellow Birch

Aspen

Maple

Sycamore

Spruce

Environment

Location / GPS: _____ Date _____

Season: ◯ Spring ◯ Summer ◯ Fall ◯ Winter

Surroundings: ◯ Hedgerows ◯ Field ◯ Park ◯ Woodland ◯ Water
◯ Other_____

Setting: ◯ Natural ◯ Artificial   Type: ◯ Evergreen ◯ Deciduous

Notes: _____
_____

General

Shape: ◯ Vase ◯ Columnar ◯ Round ◯ (Other) _____

Features: ◯ Conical/Spire ◯ Spreading ◯ Upright ◯ Weeping
◯ (Other) _____

Branching: ◯ Opposite ◯ Alternate   Estimated Age: _____

Notes: _____
_____

Needles or Leaves

Type: ◯ Needle ◯ Simple Broadleaf ◯ Compound Broadleaf ◯ Scales

Shape: ◯ Cordate (heart-shaped) ◯ Lanceolate (long and narrow)
◯ Deltoid (triangular) ◯ Obicular (round) ◯ Ovate (egg-shaped)
◯ Palm and Maple ◯ Lobed

Structure: ◯ Simple (attached to twigs or twig stems)
◯ Compound (attached to single lead steam)

Notes: _____
_____

Flowers, Fruits & Seeds

Flower Type: ◯ Single Blooms ◯ Clustered Blooms ◯ Catkins

Fruits / Seeds: ◯ Berries ◯ Apples ◯ Pears ◯ Nuts ◯ Acorns
◯ Cones ◯ Capsules ◯ Catkins ◯ (Other) _____

Notes: _____
_____

Leaf Buds & Twigs

Bud Type: ◯ Terminal (grows at tip of a shoot causing shoot to grow longer)
◯ Lateral (grow along sides of a shoot causing sideways growth)

Twig Features: ◯ Smooth ◯ Hairy ◯ Spines ◯ Corky Ribs
◯ (Other) _____

Notes: _____

Bark

Texture: ◯ Furrowed ◯ Scaly ◯ Peeling ◯ Smooth ◯ Shiny
◯ Fissured ◯ Ridges / Depressions ◯ Papery ◯ Warty
◯ (Other) _____

Color: ◯ Gray ◯ Brown ◯ Cinnamon ◯ White ◯ Silver
◯ Green ◯ Copper ◯ (Other) _____

Notes: _____

Ash

Sassafras

American Beech

Elm

Eastern White Pine

Tulip

Catalpa

Fir

Yellow Birch

Aspen

Maple

Sycamore

Spruce

Ash

Sassafras

American Beech

Elm

Eastern White Pine

Tulip

Catalpa

Fir

Yellow Birch

Aspen

Maple

Sycamore

Spruce

Environment

Location / GPS: _____ Date _____

Season: ○ Spring ○ Summer ○ Fall ○ Winter

Surroundings: ○ Hedgerows ○ Field ○ Park ○ Woodland ○ Water
○ Other_____

Setting: ○ Natural ○ Artificial   Type: ○ Evergreen ○ Deciduous

Notes: _____
_____

General

Shape: ○ Vase ○ Columnar ○ Round ○ (Other) _____

Features: ○ Conical/Spire ○ Spreading ○ Upright ○ Weeping
○ (Other) _____

Branching: ○ Opposite ○ Alternate   Estimated Age: _____

Notes: _____
_____

Needles or Leaves

Type: ○ Needle ○ Simple Broadleaf ○ Compound Broadleaf ○ Scales

Shape: ○ Cordate (heart-shaped) ○ Lanceolate (long and narrow)
○ Deltoid (triangular) ○ Obicular (round) ○ Ovate (egg-shaped)
○ Palm and Maple ○ Lobed

Structure: ○ Simple (attached to twigs or twig stems)
○ Compound (attached to single lead steam)

Notes: _____
_____

Flowers, Fruits & Seeds

Flower Type: ○ Single Blooms ○ Clustered Blooms ○ Catkins

Fruits / Seeds: ○ Berries ○ Apples ○ Pears ○ Nuts ○ Acorns
○ Cones ○ Capsules ○ Catkins ○ (Other) _____

Notes: _____
_____

Leaf Buds & Twigs

Bud Type: ○ Terminal (grows at tip of a shoot causing shoot to grow longer)
○ Lateral (grow along sides of a shoot causing sideways growth)

Twig Features: ○ Smooth ○ Hairy ○ Spines ○ Corky Ribs
○ (Other) _____

Notes: _____

Bark

Texture: ○ Furrowed ○ Scaly ○ Peeling ○ Smooth ○ Shiny
○ Fissured ○ Ridges / Depressions ○ Papery ○ Warty
○ (Other) _____

Color: ○ Gray ○ Brown ○ Cinnamon ○ White ○ Silver
○ Green ○ Copper ○ (Other) _____

Notes: _____

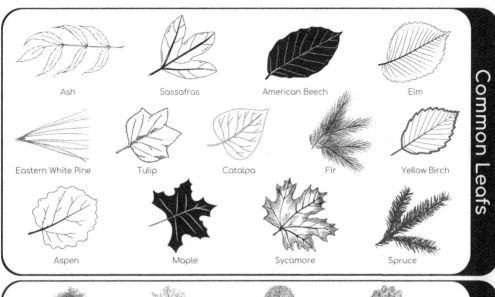

Ash · Sassafras · American Beech · Elm · Eastern White Pine · Tulip · Catalpa · Fir · Yellow Birch · Aspen · Maple · Sycamore · Spruce

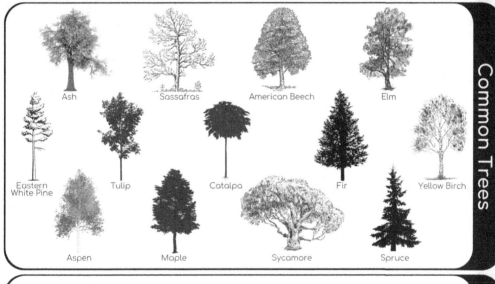

Ash · Sassafras · American Beech · Elm · Eastern White Pine · Tulip · Catalpa · Fir · Yellow Birch · Aspen · Maple · Sycamore · Spruce

Environment

Location / GPS: _____ Date _____

Season: ○ Spring ○ Summer ○ Fall ○ Winter

Surroundings: ○ Hedgerows ○ Field ○ Park ○ Woodland ○ Water
○ Other _____

Setting: ○ Natural ○ Artificial   Type: ○ Evergreen ○ Deciduous

Notes: _____
_____

General

Shape: ○ Vase ○ Columnar ○ Round ○ (Other) _____

Features: ○ Conical/Spire ○ Spreading ○ Upright ○ Weeping
○ (Other) _____

Branching: ○ Opposite ○ Alternate   Estimated Age: _____

Notes: _____
_____

Needles or Leaves

Type: ○ Needle ○ Simple Broadleaf ○ Compound Broadleaf ○ Scales

Shape: ○ Cordate (heart-shaped) ○ Lanceolate (long and narrow)
○ Deltoid (triangular) ○ Obicular (round) ○ Ovate (egg-shaped)
○ Palm and Maple ○ Lobed

Structure: ○ Simple (attached to twigs or twig stems)
○ Compound (attached to single lead steam)

Notes: _____
_____

Flowers, Fruits & Seeds

Flower Type: ○ Single Blooms ○ Clustered Blooms ○ Catkins

Fruits / Seeds: ○ Berries ○ Apples ○ Pears ○ Nuts ○ Acorns
○ Cones ○ Capsules ○ Catkins ○ (Other) _____

Notes: _____
_____

Leaf Buds & Twigs

Bud Type: ○ Terminal (grows at tip of a shoot causing shoot to grow longer)
○ Lateral (grow along sides of a shoot causing sideways growth)

Twig Features: ○ Smooth ○ Hairy ○ Spines ○ Corky Ribs
○ (Other) _____

Notes: _____

Bark

Texture: ○ Furrowed ○ Scaly ○ Peeling ○ Smooth ○ Shiny
○ Fissured ○ Ridges / Depressions ○ Papery ○ Warty
○ (Other) _____

Color: ○ Gray ○ Brown ○ Cinnamon ○ White ○ Silver
○ Green ○ Copper ○ (Other) _____

Notes: _____

Ash

Sassafras

American Beech

Elm

Eastern White Pine

Tulip

Catalpa

Fir

Yellow Birch

Aspen

Maple

Sycamore

Spruce

Ash

Sassafras

American Beech

Elm

Eastern White Pine

Tulip

Catalpa

Fir

Yellow Birch

Aspen

Maple

Sycamore

Spruce

Environment

Location / GPS: _____ Date _____

Season: ○ Spring ○ Summer ○ Fall ○ Winter

Surroundings: ○ Hedgerows ○ Field ○ Park ○ Woodland ○ Water
○ Other _____

Setting: ○ Natural ○ Artificial **Type:** ○ Evergreen ○ Deciduous

Notes: _____
_____

General

Shape: ○ Vase ○ Columnar ○ Round ○ (Other) _____

Features: ○ Conical/Spire ○ Spreading ○ Upright ○ Weeping
○ (Other) _____

Branching: ○ Opposite ○ Alternate **Estimated Age:** _____

Notes: _____
_____

Needles or Leaves

Type: ○ Needle ○ Simple Broadleaf ○ Compound Broadleaf ○ Scales

Shape: ○ Cordate (heart-shaped) ○ Lanceolate (long and narrow)
○ Deltoid (triangular) ○ Obicular (round) ○ Ovate (egg-shaped)
○ Palm and Maple ○ Lobed

Structure: ○ Simple (attached to twigs or twig stems)
○ Compound (attached to single lead steam)

Notes: _____
_____

Flowers, Fruits & Seeds

Flower Type: ○ Single Blooms ○ Clustered Blooms ○ Catkins

Fruits / Seeds: ○ Berries ○ Apples ○ Pears ○ Nuts ○ Acorns
○ Cones ○ Capsules ○ Catkins ○ (Other) _____

Notes: _____
_____

Leaf Buds & Twigs

Bud Type: ○ Terminal (grows at tip of a shoot causing shoot to grow longer)
○ Lateral (grow along sides of a shoot causing sideways growth)

Twig Features: ○ Smooth ○ Hairy ○ Spines ○ Corky Ribs
○ (Other) _____

Notes: _____

Bark

Texture: ○ Furrowed ○ Scaly ○ Peeling ○ Smooth ○ Shiny
○ Fissured ○ Ridges / Depressions ○ Papery ○ Warty
○ (Other) _____

Color: ○ Gray ○ Brown ○ Cinnamon ○ White ○ Silver
○ Green ○ Copper ○ (Other) _____

Notes: _____

Ash

Sassafras

American Beech

Elm

Eastern White Pine

Tulip

Catalpa

Fir

Yellow Birch

Aspen

Maple

Sycamore

Spruce

Ash

Sassafras

American Beech

Elm

Eastern White Pine

Tulip

Catalpa

Fir

Yellow Birch

Aspen

Maple

Sycamore

Spruce

Environment

Location / GPS: _____ Date _____

Season: ○ Spring ○ Summer ○ Fall ○ Winter

Surroundings: ○ Hedgerows ○ Field ○ Park ○ Woodland ○ Water
○ Other_____

Setting: ○ Natural ○ Artificial   Type: ○ Evergreen ○ Deciduous

Notes: _____
_____

General

Shape: ○ Vase ○ Columnar ○ Round ○ (Other) _____

Features: ○ Conical/Spire ○ Spreading ○ Upright ○ Weeping
○ (Other) _____

Branching: ○ Opposite ○ Alternate   Estimated Age: _____

Notes: _____
_____

Needles or Leaves

Type: ○ Needle ○ Simple Broadleaf ○ Compound Broadleaf ○ Scales

Shape: ○ Cordate (heart-shaped) ○ Lanceolate (long and narrow)
○ Deltoid (triangular) ○ Obicular (round) ○ Ovate (egg-shaped)
○ Palm and Maple ○ Lobed

Structure: ○ Simple (attached to twigs or twig stems)
○ Compound (attached to single lead steam)

Notes: _____
_____

Flowers, Fruits & Seeds

Flower Type: ○ Single Blooms ○ Clustered Blooms ○ Catkins

Fruits / Seeds: ○ Berries ○ Apples ○ Pears ○ Nuts ○ Acorns
○ Cones ○ Capsules ○ Catkins ○ (Other) _____

Notes: _____
_____

Leaf Buds & Twigs

Bud Type: ○ Terminal (grows at tip of a shoot causing shoot to grow longer)
○ Lateral (grow along sides of a shoot causing sideways growth)

Twig Features: ○ Smooth ○ Hairy ○ Spines ○ Corky Ribs
○ (Other) _____

Notes: _____

Bark

Texture: ○ Furrowed ○ Scaly ○ Peeling ○ Smooth ○ Shiny
○ Fissured ○ Ridges / Depressions ○ Papery ○ Warty
○ (Other) _____

Color: ○ Gray ○ Brown ○ Cinnamon ○ White ○ Silver
○ Green ○ Copper ○ (Other) _____

Notes: _____

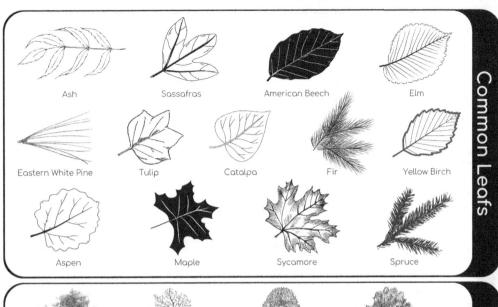

Ash

Sassafras

American Beech

Elm

Eastern White Pine

Tulip

Catalpa

Fir

Yellow Birch

Aspen

Maple

Sycamore

Spruce

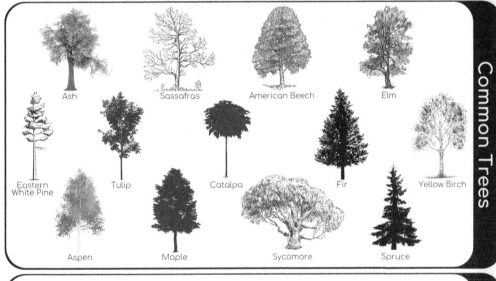

Ash

Sassafras

American Beech

Elm

Eastern White Pine

Tulip

Catalpa

Fir

Yellow Birch

Aspen

Maple

Sycamore

Spruce

Environment

Location / GPS: _____ Date _____

Season: ○ Spring ○ Summer ○ Fall ○ Winter

Surroundings: ○ Hedgerows ○ Field ○ Park ○ Woodland ○ Water
○ Other _____

Setting: ○ Natural ○ Artificial **Type:** ○ Evergreen ○ Deciduous

Notes: _____
_____

General

Shape: ○ Vase ○ Columnar ○ Round ○ (Other) _____

Features: ○ Conical/Spire ○ Spreading ○ Upright ○ Weeping
○ (Other) _____

Branching: ○ Opposite ○ Alternate **Estimated Age:** _____

Notes: _____
_____

Needles or Leaves

Type: ○ Needle ○ Simple Broadleaf ○ Compound Broadleaf ○ Scales

Shape: ○ Cordate (heart-shaped) ○ Lanceolate (long and narrow)
○ Deltoid (triangular) ○ Obicular (round) ○ Ovate (egg-shaped)
○ Palm and Maple ○ Lobed

Structure: ○ Simple (attached to twigs or twig stems)
○ Compound (attached to single lead steam)

Notes: _____
_____

Flowers, Fruits & Seeds

Flower Type: ○ Single Blooms ○ Clustered Blooms ○ Catkins

Fruits / Seeds: ○ Berries ○ Apples ○ Pears ○ Nuts ○ Acorns
○ Cones ○ Capsules ○ Catkins ○ (Other) _____

Notes: _____
_____

Leaf Buds & Twigs

Bud Type: ○ Terminal (grows at tip of a shoot causing shoot to grow longer)
○ Lateral (grow along sides of a shoot causing sideways growth)

Twig Features: ○ Smooth ○ Hairy ○ Spines ○ Corky Ribs
○ (Other) _____

Notes: _____

Bark

Texture: ○ Furrowed ○ Scaly ○ Peeling ○ Smooth ○ Shiny
○ Fissured ○ Ridges / Depressions ○ Papery ○ Warty
○ (Other) _____

Color: ○ Gray ○ Brown ○ Cinnamon ○ White ○ Silver
○ Green ○ Copper ○ (Other) _____

Notes: _____

Ash

Sassafras

American Beech

Elm

Eastern White Pine

Tulip

Catalpa

Fir

Yellow Birch

Aspen

Maple

Sycamore

Spruce

Ash

Sassafras

American Beech

Elm

Eastern White Pine

Tulip

Catalpa

Fir

Yellow Birch

Aspen

Maple

Sycamore

Spruce

Environment

Location / GPS: _____ Date _____

Season: ⚪ Spring ⚪ Summer ⚪ Fall ⚪ Winter

Surroundings: ⚪ Hedgerows ⚪ Field ⚪ Park ⚪ Woodland ⚪ Water
⚪ Other_____

Setting: ⚪ Natural ⚪ Artificial **Type:** ⚪ Evergreen ⚪ Deciduous

Notes: _____
_____

General

Shape: ⚪ Vase ⚪ Columnar ⚪ Round ⚪ (Other) _____

Features: ⚪ Conical/Spire ⚪ Spreading ⚪ Upright ⚪ Weeping
⚪ (Other) _____

Branching: ⚪ Opposite ⚪ Alternate **Estimated Age:** _____

Notes: _____
_____

Needles or Leaves

Type: ⚪ Needle ⚪ Simple Broadleaf ⚪ Compound Broadleaf ⚪ Scales

Shape: ⚪ Cordate (heart-shaped) ⚪ Lanceolate (long and narrow)
⚪ Deltoid (triangular) ⚪ Obicular (round) ⚪ Ovate (egg-shaped)
⚪ Palm and Maple ⚪ Lobed

Structure: ⚪ Simple (attached to twigs or twig stems)
⚪ Compound (attached to single lead steam)

Notes: _____
_____

Flowers, Fruits & Seeds

Flower Type: ⚪ Single Blooms ⚪ Clustered Blooms ⚪ Catkins

Fruits / Seeds: ⚪ Berries ⚪ Apples ⚪ Pears ⚪ Nuts ⚪ Acorns
⚪ Cones ⚪ Capsules ⚪ Catkins ⚪ (Other) _____

Notes: _____
_____

Leaf Buds & Twigs

Bud Type: ⚪ Terminal (grows at tip of a shoot causing shoot to grow longer)
⚪ Lateral (grow along sides of a shoot causing sideways growth)

Twig Features: ⚪ Smooth ⚪ Hairy ⚪ Spines ⚪ Corky Ribs
⚪ (Other) _____

Notes: _____

Bark

Texture: ⚪ Furrowed ⚪ Scaly ⚪ Peeling ⚪ Smooth ⚪ Shiny
⚪ Fissured ⚪ Ridges / Depressions ⚪ Papery ⚪ Warty
⚪ (Other) _____

Color: ⚪ Gray ⚪ Brown ⚪ Cinnamon ⚪ White ⚪ Silver
⚪ Green ⚪ Copper ⚪ (Other) _____

Notes: _____

Ash

Sassafras

American Beech

Elm

Eastern White Pine

Tulip

Catalpa

Fir

Yellow Birch

Aspen

Maple

Sycamore

Spruce

Ash

Sassafras

American Beech

Elm

Eastern White Pine

Tulip

Catalpa

Fir

Yellow Birch

Aspen

Maple

Sycamore

Spruce

Environment

Location / GPS: _____ Date _____

Season: ○ Spring   ○ Summer   ○ Fall   ○ Winter

Surroundings: ○ Hedgerows ○ Field ○ Park ○ Woodland ○ Water
○ Other_____

Setting: ○ Natural ○ Artificial   **Type:** ○ Evergreen ○ Deciduous

Notes: _____
_____

General

Shape: ○ Vase ○ Columnar ○ Round ○ (Other) _____

Features: ○ Conical/Spire ○ Spreading ○ Upright ○ Weeping
○ (Other) _____

Branching: ○ Opposite ○ Alternate   **Estimated Age:** _____

Notes: _____
_____

Needles or Leaves

Type: ○ Needle ○ Simple Broadleaf ○ Compound Broadleaf ○ Scales

Shape: ○ Cordate (heart-shaped) ○ Lanceolate (long and narrow)
○ Deltoid (triangular) ○ Obicular (round) ○ Ovate (egg-shaped)
○ Palm and Maple ○ Lobed

Structure: ○ Simple (attached to twigs or twig stems)
○ Compound (attached to single lead steam)

Notes: _____
_____

Flowers, Fruits & Seeds

Flower Type: ○ Single Blooms ○ Clustered Blooms ○ Catkins

Fruits / Seeds: ○ Berries ○ Apples ○ Pears ○ Nuts ○ Acorns
○ Cones ○ Capsules ○ Catkins ○ (Other) _____

Notes: _____
_____

Leaf Buds & Twigs

Bud Type: ○ Terminal (grows at tip of a shoot causing shoot to grow longer)
○ Lateral (grow along sides of a shoot causing sideways growth)

Twig Features: ○ Smooth ○ Hairy ○ Spines ○ Corky Ribs
○ (Other) _____

Notes: _____

Bark

Texture: ○ Furrowed ○ Scaly ○ Peeling ○ Smooth ○ Shiny
○ Fissured ○ Ridges / Depressions ○ Papery ○ Warty
○ (Other) _____

Color: ○ Gray ○ Brown ○ Cinnamon ○ White ○ Silver
○ Green ○ Copper ○ (Other) _____

Notes: _____

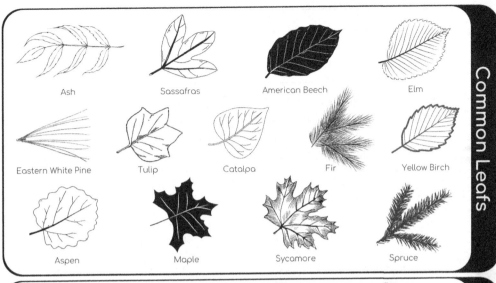

Ash

Sassafras

American Beech

Elm

Eastern White Pine

Tulip

Catalpa

Fir

Yellow Birch

Aspen

Maple

Sycamore

Spruce

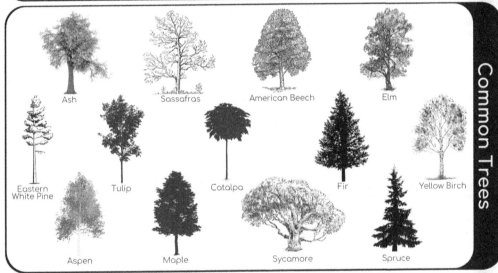

Ash

Sassafras

American Beech

Elm

Eastern White Pine

Tulip

Catalpa

Fir

Yellow Birch

Aspen

Maple

Sycamore

Spruce

Environment

Location / GPS: _____ Date _____

Season: ◯ Spring ◯ Summer ◯ Fall ◯ Winter

Surroundings: ◯ Hedgerows ◯ Field ◯ Park ◯ Woodland ◯ Water
◯ Other_____

Setting: ◯ Natural ◯ Artificial **Type:** ◯ Evergreen ◯ Deciduous

Notes: _____
_____

General

Shape: ◯ Vase ◯ Columnar ◯ Round ◯ (Other) _____

Features: ◯ Conical/Spire ◯ Spreading ◯ Upright ◯ Weeping
◯ (Other) _____

Branching: ◯ Opposite ◯ Alternate **Estimated Age:** _____

Notes: _____
_____

Needles or Leaves

Type: ◯ Needle ◯ Simple Broadleaf ◯ Compound Broadleaf ◯ Scales

Shape: ◯ Cordate (heart-shaped) ◯ Lanceolate (long and narrow)
◯ Deltoid (triangular) ◯ Obicular (round) ◯ Ovate (egg-shaped)
◯ Palm and Maple ◯ Lobed

Structure: ◯ Simple (attached to twigs or twig stems)
◯ Compound (attached to single lead steam)

Notes: _____
_____

Flowers, Fruits & Seeds

Flower Type: ◯ Single Blooms ◯ Clustered Blooms ◯ Catkins

Fruits / Seeds: ◯ Berries ◯ Apples ◯ Pears ◯ Nuts ◯ Acorns
◯ Cones ◯ Capsules ◯ Catkins ◯ (Other) _____

Notes: _____
_____

Leaf Buds & Twigs

Bud Type: ◯ Terminal (grows at tip of a shoot causing shoot to grow longer)
◯ Lateral (grow along sides of a shoot causing sideways growth)

Twig Features: ◯ Smooth ◯ Hairy ◯ Spines ◯ Corky Ribs
◯ (Other) _____

Notes: _____

Bark

Texture: ◯ Furrowed ◯ Scaly ◯ Peeling ◯ Smooth ◯ Shiny
◯ Fissured ◯ Ridges / Depressions ◯ Papery ◯ Warty
◯ (Other) _____

Color: ◯ Gray ◯ Brown ◯ Cinnamon ◯ White ◯ Silver
◯ Green ◯ Copper ◯ (Other) _____

Notes: _____

Ash

Sassafras

American Beech

Elm

Eastern White Pine

Tulip

Catalpa

Fir

Yellow Birch

Aspen

Maple

Sycamore

Spruce

Ash

Sassafras

American Beech

Elm

Eastern White Pine

Tulip

Catalpa

Fir

Yellow Birch

Aspen

Maple

Sycamore

Spruce

Environment

Location / GPS: _____ Date _____

Season: ◯ Spring ◯ Summer ◯ Fall ◯ Winter

Surroundings: ◯ Hedgerows ◯ Field ◯ Park ◯ Woodland ◯ Water
◯ Other_____

Setting: ◯ Natural ◯ Artificial **Type:** ◯ Evergreen ◯ Deciduous

Notes: _____
_____

General

Shape: ◯ Vase ◯ Columnar ◯ Round ◯ (Other) _____

Features: ◯ Conical/Spire ◯ Spreading ◯ Upright ◯ Weeping
◯ (Other) _____

Branching: ◯ Opposite ◯ Alternate **Estimated Age:** _____

Notes: _____
_____

Needles or Leaves

Type: ◯ Needle ◯ Simple Broadleaf ◯ Compound Broadleaf ◯ Scales

Shape: ◯ Cordate (heart-shaped) ◯ Lanceolate (long and narrow)
◯ Deltoid (triangular) ◯ Obicular (round) ◯ Ovate (egg-shaped)
◯ Palm and Maple ◯ Lobed

Structure: ◯ Simple (attached to twigs or twig stems)
◯ Compound (attached to single lead steam)

Notes: _____
_____

Flowers, Fruits & Seeds

Flower Type: ◯ Single Blooms ◯ Clustered Blooms ◯ Catkins

Fruits / Seeds: ◯ Berries ◯ Apples ◯ Pears ◯ Nuts ◯ Acorns
◯ Cones ◯ Capsules ◯ Catkins ◯ (Other) _____

Notes: _____
_____

Leaf Buds & Twigs

Bud Type: ◯ Terminal (grows at tip of a shoot causing shoot to grow longer)
◯ Lateral (grow along sides of a shoot causing sideways growth)

Twig Features: ◯ Smooth ◯ Hairy ◯ Spines ◯ Corky Ribs
◯ (Other) _____

Notes: _____

Bark

Texture: ◯ Furrowed ◯ Scaly ◯ Peeling ◯ Smooth ◯ Shiny
◯ Fissured ◯ Ridges / Depressions ◯ Papery ◯ Warty
◯ (Other) _____

Color: ◯ Gray ◯ Brown ◯ Cinnamon ◯ White ◯ Silver
◯ Green ◯ Copper ◯ (Other) _____

Notes: _____

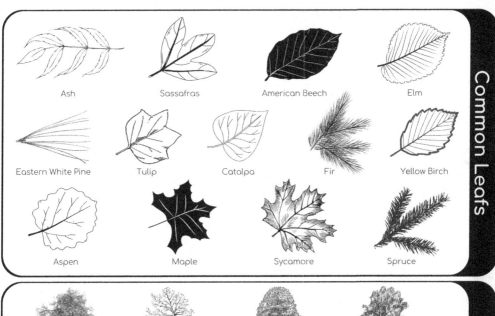

Ash   Sassafras   American Beech   Elm

Eastern White Pine   Tulip   Catalpa   Fir   Yellow Birch

Aspen   Maple   Sycamore   Spruce

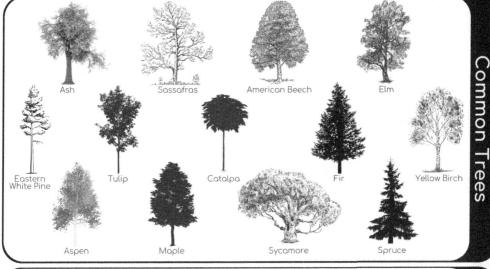

Ash   Sassafras   American Beech   Elm

Eastern White Pine   Tulip   Catalpa   Fir   Yellow Birch

Aspen   Maple   Sycamore   Spruce

Environment

Location / GPS: _____ Date _____

Season: ○ Spring ○ Summer ○ Fall ○ Winter

Surroundings: ○ Hedgerows ○ Field ○ Park ○ Woodland ○ Water
○ Other_____

Setting: ○ Natural ○ Artificial   Type: ○ Evergreen ○ Deciduous

Notes: _____
_____

General

Shape: ○ Vase ○ Columnar ○ Round ○ (Other) _____

Features: ○ Conical/Spire ○ Spreading ○ Upright ○ Weeping
○ (Other) _____

Branching: ○ Opposite ○ Alternate   Estimated Age: _____

Notes: _____
_____

Needles or Leaves

Type: ○ Needle ○ Simple Broadleaf ○ Compound Broadleaf ○ Scales

Shape: ○ Cordate (heart-shaped) ○ Lanceolate (long and narrow)
○ Deltoid (triangular) ○ Obicular (round) ○ Ovate (egg-shaped)
○ Palm and Maple ○ Lobed

Structure: ○ Simple (attached to twigs or twig stems)
○ Compound (attached to single lead steam)

Notes: _____
_____

Flowers, Fruits & Seeds

Flower Type: ○ Single Blooms ○ Clustered Blooms ○ Catkins

Fruits / Seeds: ○ Berries ○ Apples ○ Pears ○ Nuts ○ Acorns
○ Cones ○ Capsules ○ Catkins ○ (Other) _____

Notes: _____
_____

Leaf Buds & Twigs

Bud Type: ○ Terminal (grows at tip of a shoot causing shoot to grow longer)
○ Lateral (grow along sides of a shoot causing sideways growth)

Twig Features: ○ Smooth ○ Hairy ○ Spines ○ Corky Ribs
○ (Other) _____

Notes: _____

Bark

Texture: ○ Furrowed ○ Scaly ○ Peeling ○ Smooth ○ Shiny
○ Fissured ○ Ridges / Depressions ○ Papery ○ Warty
○ (Other) _____

Color: ○ Gray ○ Brown ○ Cinnamon ○ White ○ Silver
○ Green ○ Copper ○ (Other) _____

Notes: _____

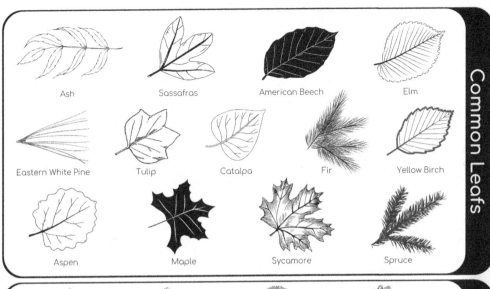

Ash

Sassafras

American Beech

Elm

Eastern White Pine

Tulip

Catalpa

Fir

Yellow Birch

Aspen

Maple

Sycamore

Spruce

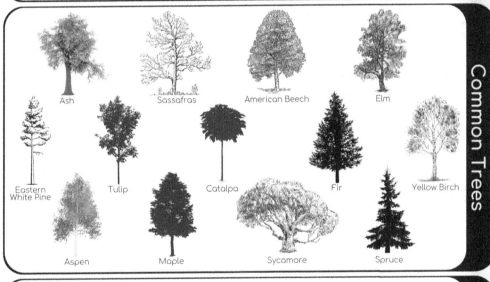

Ash

Sassafras

American Beech

Elm

Eastern White Pine

Tulip

Catalpa

Fir

Yellow Birch

Aspen

Maple

Sycamore

Spruce

Environment

Location / GPS: _____ Date _____

Season: ⚪ Spring ⚪ Summer ⚪ Fall ⚪ Winter

Surroundings: ⚪ Hedgerows ⚪ Field ⚪ Park ⚪ Woodland ⚪ Water
⚪ Other _____

Setting: ⚪ Natural ⚪ Artificial   Type: ⚪ Evergreen ⚪ Deciduous

Notes: _____
_____

General

Shape: ⚪ Vase ⚪ Columnar ⚪ Round ⚪ (Other) _____

Features: ⚪ Conical/Spire ⚪ Spreading ⚪ Upright ⚪ Weeping
⚪ (Other) _____

Branching: ⚪ Opposite ⚪ Alternate   Estimated Age: _____

Notes: _____
_____

Needles or Leaves

Type: ⚪ Needle ⚪ Simple Broadleaf ⚪ Compound Broadleaf ⚪ Scales

Shape: ⚪ Cordate (heart-shaped) ⚪ Lanceolate (long and narrow)
⚪ Deltoid (triangular) ⚪ Obicular (round) ⚪ Ovate (egg-shaped)
⚪ Palm and Maple ⚪ Lobed

Structure: ⚪ Simple (attached to twigs or twig stems)
⚪ Compound (attached to single lead steam)

Notes: _____
_____

Flowers, Fruits & Seeds

Flower Type: ⚪ Single Blooms ⚪ Clustered Blooms ⚪ Catkins

Fruits / Seeds: ⚪ Berries ⚪ Apples ⚪ Pears ⚪ Nuts ⚪ Acorns
⚪ Cones ⚪ Capsules ⚪ Catkins ⚪ (Other) _____

Notes: _____
_____

Leaf Buds & Twigs

Bud Type: ⚪ Terminal (grows at tip of a shoot causing shoot to grow longer)
⚪ Lateral (grow along sides of a shoot causing sideways growth)

Twig Features: ⚪ Smooth ⚪ Hairy ⚪ Spines ⚪ Corky Ribs
⚪ (Other) _____

Notes: _____

Bark

Texture: ⚪ Furrowed ⚪ Scaly ⚪ Peeling ⚪ Smooth ⚪ Shiny
⚪ Fissured ⚪ Ridges / Depressions ⚪ Papery ⚪ Warty
⚪ (Other) _____

Color: ⚪ Gray ⚪ Brown ⚪ Cinnamon ⚪ White ⚪ Silver
⚪ Green ⚪ Copper ⚪ (Other) _____

Notes: _____

Ash
Sassafras
American Beech
Elm

Eastern White Pine
Tulip
Catalpa
Fir
Yellow Birch

Aspen
Maple
Sycamore
Spruce

Ash
Sassafras
American Beech
Elm

Eastern White Pine
Tulip
Catalpa
Fir
Yellow Birch

Aspen
Maple
Sycamore
Spruce

Environment

Location / GPS: _____ Date _____

Season: ○ Spring ○ Summer ○ Fall ○ Winter

Surroundings: ○ Hedgerows ○ Field ○ Park ○ Woodland ○ Water
○ Other_____

Setting: ○ Natural ○ Artificial   Type: ○ Evergreen ○ Deciduous

Notes:_____
_____

General

Shape: ○ Vase ○ Columnar ○ Round ○ (Other) _____

Features: ○ Conical/Spire ○ Spreading ○ Upright ○ Weeping
○ (Other) _____

Branching: ○ Opposite ○ Alternate   Estimated Age: _____

Notes: _____
_____

Needles or Leaves

Type: ○ Needle ○ Simple Broadleaf ○ Compound Broadleaf ○ Scales

Shape: ○ Cordate (heart-shaped) ○ Lanceolate (long and narrow)
○ Deltoid (triangular) ○ Obicular (round) ○ Ovate (egg-shaped)
○ Palm and Maple ○ Lobed

Structure: ○ Simple (attached to twigs or twig stems)
○ Compound (attached to single lead steam)

Notes: _____
_____

Flowers, Fruits & Seeds

Flower Type: ○ Single Blooms ○ Clustered Blooms ○ Catkins

Fruits / Seeds: ○ Berries ○ Apples ○ Pears ○ Nuts ○ Acorns
○ Cones ○ Capsules ○ Catkins ○ (Other) _____

Notes: _____
_____

Leaf Buds & Twigs

Bud Type: ○ Terminal (grows at tip of a shoot causing shoot to grow longer)
○ Lateral (grow along sides of a shoot causing sideways growth)

Twig Features: ○ Smooth ○ Hairy ○ Spines ○ Corky Ribs
○ (Other) _____

Notes: _____

Bark

Texture: ○ Furrowed ○ Scaly ○ Peeling ○ Smooth ○ Shiny
○ Fissured ○ Ridges / Depressions ○ Papery ○ Warty
○ (Other) _____

Color: ○ Gray ○ Brown ○ Cinnamon ○ White ○ Silver
○ Green ○ Copper ○ (Other) _____

Notes: _____

Ash

Sassafras

American Beech

Elm

Eastern White Pine

Tulip

Catalpa

Fir

Yellow Birch

Aspen

Maple

Sycamore

Spruce

Ash

Sassafras

American Beech

Elm

Eastern White Pine

Tulip

Catalpa

Fir

Yellow Birch

Aspen

Maple

Sycamore

Spruce

Environment

Location / GPS: _____ Date _____

Season: ○ Spring   ○ Summer   ○ Fall   ○ Winter

Surroundings: ○ Hedgerows   ○ Field   ○ Park   ○ Woodland   ○ Water
○ Other_____

Setting: ○ Natural   ○ Artificial   Type: ○ Evergreen   ○ Deciduous

Notes: _____
_____

General

Shape: ○ Vase   ○ Columnar   ○ Round   ○ (Other) _____

Features: ○ Conical/Spire   ○ Spreading   ○ Upright   ○ Weeping
○ (Other) _____

Branching: ○ Opposite   ○ Alternate   Estimated Age: _____

Notes: _____
_____

Needles or Leaves

Type: ○ Needle   ○ Simple Broadleaf   ○ Compound Broadleaf   ○ Scales

Shape: ○ Cordate (heart-shaped)   ○ Lanceolate (long and narrow)
○ Deltoid (triangular)   ○ Obicular (round)   ○ Ovate (egg-shaped)
○ Palm and Maple   ○ Lobed

Structure: ○ Simple (attached to twigs or twig stems)
○ Compound (attached to single lead steam)

Notes: _____
_____

Flowers, Fruits & Seeds

Flower Type: ○ Single Blooms   ○ Clustered Blooms   ○ Catkins

Fruits / Seeds: ○ Berries   ○ Apples   ○ Pears   ○ Nuts   ○ Acorns
○ Cones   ○ Capsules   ○ Catkins   ○ (Other) _____

Notes: _____
_____

Leaf Buds & Twigs

Bud Type: ○ Terminal (grows at tip of a shoot causing shoot to grow longer)
○ Lateral (grow along sides of a shoot causing sideways growth)

Twig Features: ○ Smooth   ○ Hairy   ○ Spines   ○ Corky Ribs
○ (Other) _____

Notes: _____

Bark

Texture: ○ Furrowed   ○ Scaly   ○ Peeling   ○ Smooth   ○ Shiny
○ Fissured   ○ Ridges / Depressions   ○ Papery   ○ Warty
○ (Other) _____

Color: ○ Gray   ○ Brown   ○ Cinnamon   ○ White   ○ Silver
○ Green   ○ Copper   ○ (Other) _____

Notes: _____

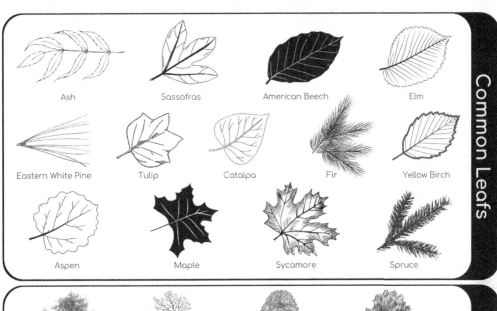

Ash

Sassafras

American Beech

Elm

Eastern White Pine

Tulip

Catalpa

Fir

Yellow Birch

Aspen

Maple

Sycamore

Spruce

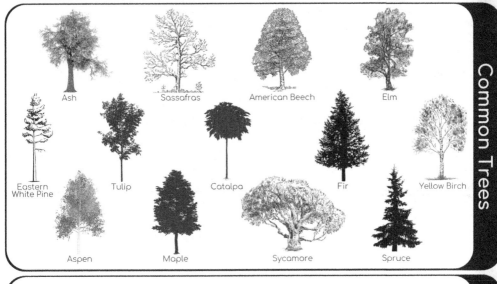

Ash

Sassafras

American Beech

Elm

Eastern White Pine

Tulip

Catalpa

Fir

Yellow Birch

Aspen

Maple

Sycamore

Spruce

Environment

Location / GPS: _____ Date _____

Season: ◯ Spring ◯ Summer ◯ Fall ◯ Winter

Surroundings: ◯ Hedgerows ◯ Field ◯ Park ◯ Woodland ◯ Water
◯ Other_____

Setting: ◯ Natural ◯ Artificial   Type: ◯ Evergreen ◯ Deciduous

Notes: _____
_____

General

Shape: ◯ Vase ◯ Columnar ◯ Round ◯ (Other) _____

Features: ◯ Conical/Spire ◯ Spreading ◯ Upright ◯ Weeping
◯ (Other) _____

Branching: ◯ Opposite ◯ Alternate   Estimated Age: _____

Notes: _____
_____

Needles or Leaves

Type: ◯ Needle ◯ Simple Broadleaf ◯ Compound Broadleaf ◯ Scales

Shape: ◯ Cordate (heart-shaped) ◯ Lanceolate (long and narrow)
◯ Deltoid (triangular) ◯ Obicular (round) ◯ Ovate (egg-shaped)
◯ Palm and Maple ◯ Lobed

Structure: ◯ Simple (attached to twigs or twig stems)
◯ Compound (attached to single lead steam)

Notes: _____
_____

Flowers, Fruits & Seeds

Flower Type: ◯ Single Blooms ◯ Clustered Blooms ◯ Catkins

Fruits / Seeds: ◯ Berries ◯ Apples ◯ Pears ◯ Nuts ◯ Acorns
◯ Cones ◯ Capsules ◯ Catkins ◯ (Other) _____

Notes: _____
_____

Leaf Buds & Twigs

Bud Type: ◯ Terminal (grows at tip of a shoot causing shoot to grow longer)
◯ Lateral (grow along sides of a shoot causing sideways growth)

Twig Features: ◯ Smooth ◯ Hairy ◯ Spines ◯ Corky Ribs
◯ (Other) _____

Notes: _____

Bark

Texture: ◯ Furrowed ◯ Scaly ◯ Peeling ◯ Smooth ◯ Shiny
◯ Fissured ◯ Ridges / Depressions ◯ Papery ◯ Warty
◯ (Other) _____

Color: ◯ Gray ◯ Brown ◯ Cinnamon ◯ White ◯ Silver
◯ Green ◯ Copper ◯ (Other) _____

Notes: _____

Ash

Sassafras

American Beech

Elm

Eastern White Pine

Tulip

Catalpa

Fir

Yellow Birch

Aspen

Maple

Sycamore

Spruce

Ash

Sassafras

American Beech

Elm

Eastern White Pine

Tulip

Catalpa

Fir

Yellow Birch

Aspen

Maple

Sycamore

Spruce

Environment

Location / GPS: _____ Date _____

Season: ◯ Spring ◯ Summer ◯ Fall ◯ Winter

Surroundings: ◯ Hedgerows ◯ Field ◯ Park ◯ Woodland ◯ Water
◯ Other_____

Setting: ◯ Natural ◯ Artificial   Type: ◯ Evergreen ◯ Deciduous

Notes:_____
_____

General

Shape: ◯ Vase ◯ Columnar ◯ Round ◯ (Other) _____

Features: ◯ Conical/Spire ◯ Spreading ◯ Upright ◯ Weeping
◯ (Other) _____

Branching: ◯ Opposite ◯ Alternate   Estimated Age: _____

Notes: _____
_____

Needles or Leaves

Type: ◯ Needle ◯ Simple Broadleaf ◯ Compound Broadleaf ◯ Scales

Shape: ◯ Cordate (heart-shaped) ◯ Lanceolate (long and narrow)
◯ Deltoid (triangular) ◯ Obicular (round) ◯ Ovate (egg-shaped)
◯ Palm and Maple ◯ Lobed

Structure: ◯ Simple (attached to twigs or twig stems)
◯ Compound (attached to single lead steam)

Notes: _____
_____

Flowers, Fruits & Seeds

Flower Type: ◯ Single Blooms ◯ Clustered Blooms ◯ Catkins

Fruits / Seeds: ◯ Berries ◯ Apples ◯ Pears ◯ Nuts ◯ Acorns
◯ Cones ◯ Capsules ◯ Catkins ◯ (Other) _____

Notes: _____
_____

Leaf Buds & Twigs

Bud Type: ◯ Terminal (grows at tip of a shoot causing shoot to grow longer)
◯ Lateral (grow along sides of a shoot causing sideways growth)

Twig Features: ◯ Smooth ◯ Hairy ◯ Spines ◯ Corky Ribs
◯ (Other) _____

Notes: _____

Bark

Texture: ◯ Furrowed ◯ Scaly ◯ Peeling ◯ Smooth ◯ Shiny
◯ Fissured ◯ Ridges / Depressions ◯ Papery ◯ Warty
◯ (Other) _____

Color: ◯ Gray ◯ Brown ◯ Cinnamon ◯ White ◯ Silver
◯ Green ◯ Copper ◯ (Other) _____

Notes: _____

Ash

Sassafras

American Beech

Elm

Eastern White Pine

Tulip

Catalpa

Fir

Yellow Birch

Aspen

Maple

Sycamore

Spruce

Ash

Sassafras

American Beech

Elm

Eastern White Pine

Tulip

Catalpa

Fir

Yellow Birch

Aspen

Maple

Sycamore

Spruce

Environment

Location / GPS: _____ Date _____

Season: ◯ Spring ◯ Summer ◯ Fall ◯ Winter

Surroundings: ◯ Hedgerows ◯ Field ◯ Park ◯ Woodland ◯ Water
◯ Other _____

Setting: ◯ Natural ◯ Artificial   Type: ◯ Evergreen ◯ Deciduous

Notes: _____
_____

General

Shape: ◯ Vase ◯ Columnar ◯ Round ◯ (Other) _____

Features: ◯ Conical/Spire ◯ Spreading ◯ Upright ◯ Weeping
◯ (Other) _____

Branching: ◯ Opposite ◯ Alternate   Estimated Age: _____

Notes: _____
_____

Needles or Leaves

Type: ◯ Needle ◯ Simple Broadleaf ◯ Compound Broadleaf ◯ Scales

Shape: ◯ Cordate (heart-shaped) ◯ Lanceolate (long and narrow)
◯ Deltoid (triangular) ◯ Obicular (round) ◯ Ovate (egg-shaped)
◯ Palm and Maple ◯ Lobed

Structure: ◯ Simple (attached to twigs or twig stems)
◯ Compound (attached to single lead steam)

Notes: _____
_____

Flowers, Fruits & Seeds

Flower Type: ◯ Single Blooms ◯ Clustered Blooms ◯ Catkins

Fruits / Seeds: ◯ Berries ◯ Apples ◯ Pears ◯ Nuts ◯ Acorns
◯ Cones ◯ Capsules ◯ Catkins ◯ (Other) _____

Notes: _____
_____

Leaf Buds & Twigs

Bud Type: ◯ Terminal (grows at tip of a shoot causing shoot to grow longer)
◯ Lateral (grow along sides of a shoot causing sideways growth)

Twig Features: ◯ Smooth ◯ Hairy ◯ Spines ◯ Corky Ribs
◯ (Other) _____

Notes: _____

Bark

Texture: ◯ Furrowed ◯ Scaly ◯ Peeling ◯ Smooth ◯ Shiny
◯ Fissured ◯ Ridges / Depressions ◯ Papery ◯ Warty
◯ (Other) _____

Color: ◯ Gray ◯ Brown ◯ Cinnamon ◯ White ◯ Silver
◯ Green ◯ Copper ◯ (Other) _____

Notes: _____

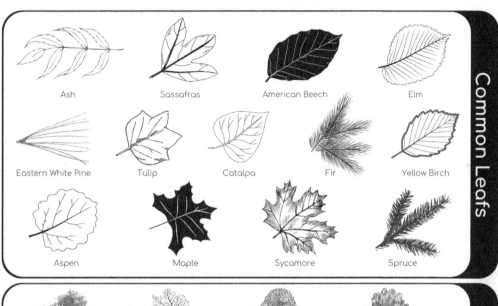

Ash
Sassafras
American Beech
Elm

Eastern White Pine
Tulip
Catalpa
Fir
Yellow Birch

Aspen
Maple
Sycamore
Spruce

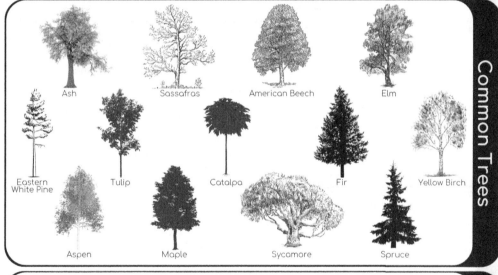

Ash
Sassafras
American Beech
Elm

Eastern White Pine
Tulip
Catalpa
Fir
Yellow Birch

Aspen
Maple
Sycamore
Spruce

Environment

Location / GPS: _____ Date _____

Season: ○ Spring ○ Summer ○ Fall ○ Winter

Surroundings: ○ Hedgerows ○ Field ○ Park ○ Woodland ○ Water
○ Other_____

Setting: ○ Natural ○ Artificial   Type: ○ Evergreen ○ Deciduous

Notes: _____
_____

General

Shape: ○ Vase ○ Columnar ○ Round ○ (Other) _____

Features: ○ Conical/Spire ○ Spreading ○ Upright ○ Weeping
○ (Other) _____

Branching: ○ Opposite ○ Alternate   Estimated Age: _____

Notes: _____
_____

Needles or Leaves

Type: ○ Needle ○ Simple Broadleaf ○ Compound Broadleaf ○ Scales

Shape: ○ Cordate (heart-shaped) ○ Lanceolate (long and narrow)
○ Deltoid (triangular) ○ Obicular (round) ○ Ovate (egg-shaped)
○ Palm and Maple ○ Lobed

Structure: ○ Simple (attached to twigs or twig stems)
○ Compound (attached to single lead steam)

Notes: _____
_____

Flowers, Fruits & Seeds

Flower Type: ○ Single Blooms ○ Clustered Blooms ○ Catkins

Fruits / Seeds: ○ Berries ○ Apples ○ Pears ○ Nuts ○ Acorns
○ Cones ○ Capsules ○ Catkins ○ (Other) _____

Notes: _____
_____

Leaf Buds & Twigs

Bud Type: ○ Terminal (grows at tip of a shoot causing shoot to grow longer)
○ Lateral (grow along sides of a shoot causing sideways growth)

Twig Features: ○ Smooth ○ Hairy ○ Spines ○ Corky Ribs
○ (Other) _____

Notes: _____

Bark

Texture: ○ Furrowed ○ Scaly ○ Peeling ○ Smooth ○ Shiny
○ Fissured ○ Ridges / Depressions ○ Papery ○ Warty
○ (Other) _____

Color: ○ Gray ○ Brown ○ Cinnamon ○ White ○ Silver
○ Green ○ Copper ○ (Other) _____

Notes: _____

Ash

Sassafras

American Beech

Elm

Eastern White Pine

Tulip

Catalpa

Fir

Yellow Birch

Aspen

Maple

Sycamore

Spruce

Ash

Sassafras

American Beech

Elm

Eastern White Pine

Tulip

Catalpa

Fir

Yellow Birch

Aspen

Maple

Sycamore

Spruce

Environment

Location / GPS: _____ Date _____

Season: ○ Spring ○ Summer ○ Fall ○ Winter

Surroundings: ○ Hedgerows ○ Field ○ Park ○ Woodland ○ Water
○ Other _____

Setting: ○ Natural ○ Artificial Type: ○ Evergreen ○ Deciduous

Notes: _____
_____

General

Shape: ○ Vase ○ Columnar ○ Round ○ (Other) _____

Features: ○ Conical/Spire ○ Spreading ○ Upright ○ Weeping
○ (Other) _____

Branching: ○ Opposite ○ Alternate Estimated Age: _____

Notes: _____
_____

Needles or Leaves

Type: ○ Needle ○ Simple Broadleaf ○ Compound Broadleaf ○ Scales

Shape: ○ Cordate (heart-shaped) ○ Lanceolate (long and narrow)
○ Deltoid (triangular) ○ Obicular (round) ○ Ovate (egg-shaped)
○ Palm and Maple ○ Lobed

Structure: ○ Simple (attached to twigs or twig stems)
○ Compound (attached to single lead steam)

Notes: _____
_____

Flowers, Fruits & Seeds

Flower Type: ○ Single Blooms ○ Clustered Blooms ○ Catkins

Fruits / Seeds: ○ Berries ○ Apples ○ Pears ○ Nuts ○ Acorns
○ Cones ○ Capsules ○ Catkins ○ (Other) _____

Notes: _____
_____

Leaf Buds & Twigs

Bud Type: ○ Terminal (grows at tip of a shoot causing shoot to grow longer)
○ Lateral (grow along sides of a shoot causing sideways growth)

Twig Features: ○ Smooth ○ Hairy ○ Spines ○ Corky Ribs
○ (Other) _____

Notes: _____

Bark

Texture: ○ Furrowed ○ Scaly ○ Peeling ○ Smooth ○ Shiny
○ Fissured ○ Ridges / Depressions ○ Papery ○ Warty
○ (Other) _____

Color: ○ Gray ○ Brown ○ Cinnamon ○ White ○ Silver
○ Green ○ Copper ○ (Other) _____

Notes: _____

Ash

Sassafras

American Beech

Elm

Eastern White Pine

Tulip

Catalpa

Fir

Yellow Birch

Aspen

Maple

Sycamore

Spruce

Ash

Sassafras

American Beech

Elm

Eastern
White Pine

Tulip

Catalpa

Fir

Yellow Birch

Aspen

Maple

Sycamore

Spruce

Environment

Location / GPS: _____ Date _____

Season: ○ Spring ○ Summer ○ Fall ○ Winter

Surroundings: ○ Hedgerows ○ Field ○ Park ○ Woodland ○ Water
○ Other_____

Setting: ○ Natural ○ Artificial **Type:** ○ Evergreen ○ Deciduous

Notes: _____
_____

General

Shape: ○ Vase ○ Columnar ○ Round ○(Other) _____

Features: ○ Conical/Spire ○ Spreading ○ Upright ○ Weeping
○(Other) _____

Branching: ○ Opposite ○ Alternate **Estimated Age:** _____

Notes: _____
_____

Needles or Leaves

Type: ○ Needle ○ Simple Broadleaf ○ Compound Broadleaf ○ Scales

Shape: ○ Cordate (heart-shaped) ○ Lanceolate (long and narrow)
○ Deltoid (triangular) ○ Obicular (round) ○ Ovate (egg-shaped)
○ Palm and Maple ○ Lobed

Structure: ○ Simple (attached to twigs or twig stems)
○ Compound (attached to single lead steam)

Notes: _____
_____

Flowers, Fruits & Seeds

Flower Type: ○ Single Blooms ○ Clustered Blooms ○ Catkins

Fruits / Seeds: ○ Berries ○ Apples ○ Pears ○ Nuts ○ Acorns
○ Cones ○ Capsules ○ Catkins ○(Other) _____

Notes: _____
_____

Leaf Buds & Twigs

Bud Type: ○ Terminal (grows at tip of a shoot causing shoot to grow longer)
○ Lateral (grow along sides of a shoot causing sideways growth)

Twig Features: ○ Smooth ○ Hairy ○ Spines ○ Corky Ribs
○(Other) _____

Notes: _____

Bark

Texture: ○ Furrowed ○ Scaly ○ Peeling ○ Smooth ○ Shiny
○ Fissured ○ Ridges / Depressions ○ Papery ○ Warty
○(Other) _____

Color: ○ Gray ○ Brown ○ Cinnamon ○ White ○ Silver
○ Green ○ Copper ○(Other) _____

Notes: _____

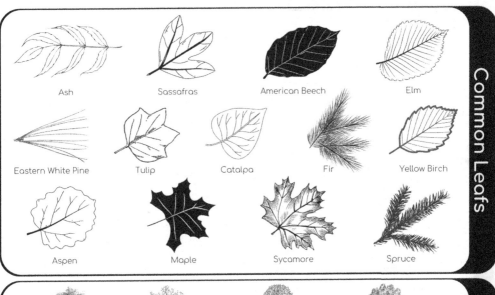

Ash Sassafras American Beech Elm

Eastern White Pine Tulip Catalpa Fir Yellow Birch

Aspen Maple Sycamore Spruce

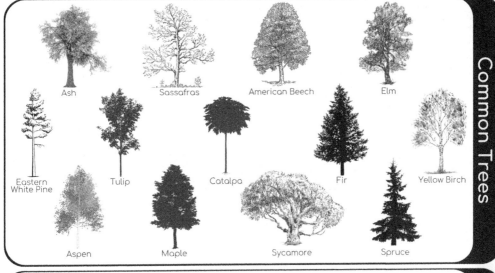

Ash Sassafras American Beech Elm

Eastern White Pine Tulip Catalpa Fir Yellow Birch

Aspen Maple Sycamore Spruce

Environment

Location / GPS: _____ Date _____

Season: ◯ Spring ◯ Summer ◯ Fall ◯ Winter

Surroundings: ◯ Hedgerows ◯ Field ◯ Park ◯ Woodland ◯ Water
◯ Other _____

Setting: ◯ Natural ◯ Artificial   Type: ◯ Evergreen ◯ Deciduous

Notes: _____
_____

General

Shape: ◯ Vase ◯ Columnar ◯ Round ◯ (Other) _____

Features: ◯ Conical/Spire ◯ Spreading ◯ Upright ◯ Weeping
◯ (Other) _____

Branching: ◯ Opposite ◯ Alternate   Estimated Age: _____

Notes: _____
_____

Needles or Leaves

Type: ◯ Needle ◯ Simple Broadleaf ◯ Compound Broadleaf ◯ Scales

Shape: ◯ Cordate (heart-shaped) ◯ Lanceolate (long and narrow)
◯ Deltoid (triangular) ◯ Obicular (round) ◯ Ovate (egg-shaped)
◯ Palm and Maple ◯ Lobed

Structure: ◯ Simple (attached to twigs or twig stems)
◯ Compound (attached to single lead steam)

Notes: _____
_____

Flowers, Fruits & Seeds

Flower Type: ◯ Single Blooms ◯ Clustered Blooms ◯ Catkins

Fruits / Seeds: ◯ Berries ◯ Apples ◯ Pears ◯ Nuts ◯ Acorns
◯ Cones ◯ Capsules ◯ Catkins ◯ (Other) _____

Notes: _____
_____

Leaf Buds & Twigs

Bud Type: ◯ Terminal (grows at tip of a shoot causing shoot to grow longer)
◯ Lateral (grow along sides of a shoot causing sideways growth)

Twig Features: ◯ Smooth ◯ Hairy ◯ Spines ◯ Corky Ribs
◯ (Other) _____

Notes: _____

Bark

Texture: ◯ Furrowed ◯ Scaly ◯ Peeling ◯ Smooth ◯ Shiny
◯ Fissured ◯ Ridges / Depressions ◯ Papery ◯ Warty
◯ (Other) _____

Color: ◯ Gray ◯ Brown ◯ Cinnamon ◯ White ◯ Silver
◯ Green ◯ Copper ◯ (Other) _____

Notes: _____

Ash

Sassafras

American Beech

Elm

Eastern White Pine

Tulip

Catalpa

Fir

Yellow Birch

Aspen

Maple

Sycamore

Spruce

Ash

Sassafras

American Beech

Elm

Eastern White Pine

Tulip

Catalpa

Fir

Yellow Birch

Aspen

Maple

Sycamore

Spruce

Environment

Location / GPS: _____ Date _____

Season: ○ Spring   ○ Summer   ○ Fall   ○ Winter

Surroundings: ○ Hedgerows ○ Field ○ Park ○ Woodland ○ Water
○ Other_____

Setting: ○ Natural   ○ Artificial   Type: ○ Evergreen   ○ Deciduous

Notes: _____
_____

General

Shape: ○ Vase ○ Columnar ○ Round ○ (Other) _____

Features: ○ Conical/Spire ○ Spreading ○ Upright ○ Weeping
○ (Other) _____

Branching: ○ Opposite ○ Alternate   Estimated Age: _____

Notes: _____
_____

Needles or Leaves

Type: ○ Needle ○ Simple Broadleaf ○ Compound Broadleaf ○ Scales

Shape: ○ Cordate (heart-shaped) ○ Lanceolate (long and narrow)
○ Deltoid (triangular) ○ Obicular (round) ○ Ovate (egg-shaped)
○ Palm and Maple ○ Lobed

Structure: ○ Simple (attached to twigs or twig stems)
○ Compound (attached to single lead steam)

Notes: _____
_____

Flowers, Fruits & Seeds

Flower Type: ○ Single Blooms ○ Clustered Blooms ○ Catkins

Fruits / Seeds: ○ Berries ○ Apples ○ Pears ○ Nuts ○ Acorns
○ Cones ○ Capsules ○ Catkins ○ (Other) _____

Notes: _____
_____

Leaf Buds & Twigs

Bud Type: ○ Terminal (grows at tip of a shoot causing shoot to grow longer)
○ Lateral (grow along sides of a shoot causing sideways growth)

Twig Features: ○ Smooth ○ Hairy ○ Spines ○ Corky Ribs
○ (Other) _____

Notes: _____

Bark

Texture: ○ Furrowed ○ Scaly ○ Peeling ○ Smooth ○ Shiny
○ Fissured ○ Ridges / Depressions ○ Papery ○ Warty
○ (Other) _____

Color: ○ Gray ○ Brown ○ Cinnamon ○ White ○ Silver
○ Green ○ Copper ○ (Other) _____

Notes: _____

Ash

Sassafras

American Beech

Elm

Eastern White Pine

Tulip

Catalpa

Fir

Yellow Birch

Aspen

Maple

Sycamore

Spruce

Ash

Sassafras

American Beech

Elm

Eastern White Pine

Tulip

Catalpa

Fir

Yellow Birch

Aspen

Maple

Sycamore

Spruce

Environment

Location / GPS: _____ Date _____

Season: ○ Spring   ○ Summer   ○ Fall   ○ Winter

Surroundings: ○ Hedgerows ○ Field ○ Park ○ Woodland ○ Water
○ Other_____

Setting: ○ Natural ○ Artificial   Type: ○ Evergreen ○ Deciduous

Notes: _____
_____

General

Shape: ○ Vase ○ Columnar ○ Round ○ (Other) _____

Features: ○ Conical/Spire ○ Spreading ○ Upright ○ Weeping
○ (Other) _____

Branching: ○ Opposite ○ Alternate   Estimated Age: _____

Notes: _____
_____

Needles or Leaves

Type: ○ Needle ○ Simple Broadleaf ○ Compound Broadleaf ○ Scales

Shape: ○ Cordate (heart-shaped) ○ Lanceolate (long and narrow)
○ Deltoid (triangular) ○ Obicular (round) ○ Ovate (egg-shaped)
○ Palm and Maple ○ Lobed

Structure: ○ Simple (attached to twigs or twig stems)
○ Compound (attached to single lead steam)

Notes: _____
_____

Flowers, Fruits & Seeds

Flower Type: ○ Single Blooms ○ Clustered Blooms ○ Catkins

Fruits / Seeds: ○ Berries ○ Apples ○ Pears ○ Nuts ○ Acorns
○ Cones ○ Capsules ○ Catkins ○ (Other) _____

Notes: _____
_____

Leaf Buds & Twigs

Bud Type: ○ Terminal (grows at tip of a shoot causing shoot to grow longer)
○ Lateral (grow along sides of a shoot causing sideways growth)

Twig Features: ○ Smooth ○ Hairy ○ Spines ○ Corky Ribs
○ (Other) _____

Notes: _____

Bark

Texture: ○ Furrowed ○ Scaly ○ Peeling ○ Smooth ○ Shiny
○ Fissured ○ Ridges / Depressions ○ Papery ○ Warty
○ (Other) _____

Color: ○ Gray ○ Brown ○ Cinnamon ○ White ○ Silver
○ Green ○ Copper ○ (Other) _____

Notes: _____

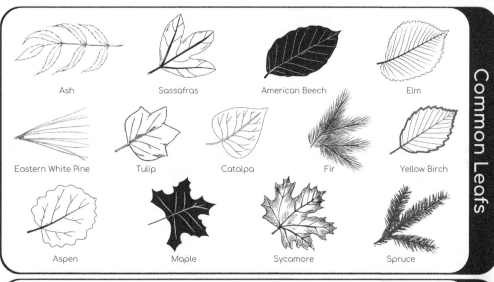

Ash | Sassafras | American Beech | Elm
Eastern White Pine | Tulip | Catalpa | Fir | Yellow Birch
Aspen | Maple | Sycamore | Spruce

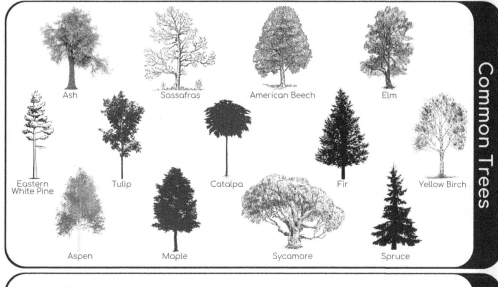

Ash | Sassafras | American Beech | Elm
Eastern White Pine | Tulip | Catalpa | Fir | Yellow Birch
Aspen | Maple | Sycamore | Spruce

Environment

Location / GPS: _____ Date _____

Season: ○ Spring ○ Summer ○ Fall ○ Winter

Surroundings: ○ Hedgerows ○ Field ○ Park ○ Woodland ○ Water
○ Other_____

Setting: ○ Natural ○ Artificial **Type:** ○ Evergreen ○ Deciduous

Notes: _____

_____

General

Shape: ○ Vase ○ Columnar ○ Round ○ (Other) _____

Features: ○ Conical/Spire ○ Spreading ○ Upright ○ Weeping
○ (Other) _____

Branching: ○ Opposite ○ Alternate **Estimated Age:** _____

Notes: _____

_____

Needles or Leaves

Type: ○ Needle ○ Simple Broadleaf ○ Compound Broadleaf ○ Scales

Shape: ○ Cordate (heart-shaped) ○ Lanceolate (long and narrow)
○ Deltoid (triangular) ○ Obicular (round) ○ Ovate (egg-shaped)
○ Palm and Maple ○ Lobed

Structure: ○ Simple (attached to twigs or twig stems)
○ Compound (attached to single lead steam)

Notes: _____

_____

Flowers, Fruits & Seeds

Flower Type: ○ Single Blooms ○ Clustered Blooms ○ Catkins

Fruits / Seeds: ○ Berries ○ Apples ○ Pears ○ Nuts ○ Acorns
○ Cones ○ Capsules ○ Catkins ○ (Other) _____

Notes: _____

_____

Leaf Buds & Twigs

Bud Type: ○ Terminal (grows at tip of a shoot causing shoot to grow longer)
○ Lateral (grow along sides of a shoot causing sideways growth)

Twig Features: ○ Smooth ○ Hairy ○ Spines ○ Corky Ribs
○ (Other) _____

Notes: _____

Bark

Texture: ○ Furrowed ○ Scaly ○ Peeling ○ Smooth ○ Shiny
○ Fissured ○ Ridges / Depressions ○ Papery ○ Warty
○ (Other) _____

Color: ○ Gray ○ Brown ○ Cinnamon ○ White ○ Silver
○ Green ○ Copper ○ (Other) _____

Notes: _____

Ash

Sassafras

American Beech

Elm

Eastern White Pine

Tulip

Catalpa

Fir

Yellow Birch

Aspen

Maple

Sycamore

Spruce

Ash

Sassafras

American Beech

Elm

Eastern White Pine

Tulip

Catalpa

Fir

Yellow Birch

Aspen

Maple

Sycamore

Spruce

Environment

Location / GPS: _____ Date _____

Season: ○ Spring ○ Summer ○ Fall ○ Winter

Surroundings: ○ Hedgerows ○ Field ○ Park ○ Woodland ○ Water
○ Other_____

Setting: ○ Natural ○ Artificial   Type: ○ Evergreen ○ Deciduous

Notes: _____
_____

General

Shape: ○ Vase ○ Columnar ○ Round ○ (Other) _____

Features: ○ Conical/Spire ○ Spreading ○ Upright ○ Weeping
○ (Other) _____

Branching: ○ Opposite ○ Alternate   Estimated Age: _____

Notes: _____
_____

Needles or Leaves

Type: ○ Needle ○ Simple Broadleaf ○ Compound Broadleaf ○ Scales

Shape: ○ Cordate (heart-shaped) ○ Lanceolate (long and narrow)
○ Deltoid (triangular) ○ Obicular (round) ○ Ovate (egg-shaped)
○ Palm and Maple ○ Lobed

Structure: ○ Simple (attached to twigs or twig stems)
○ Compound (attached to single lead steam)

Notes: _____
_____

Flowers, Fruits & Seeds

Flower Type: ○ Single Blooms ○ Clustered Blooms ○ Catkins

Fruits / Seeds: ○ Berries ○ Apples ○ Pears ○ Nuts ○ Acorns
○ Cones ○ Capsules ○ Catkins ○ (Other) _____

Notes: _____
_____

Leaf Buds & Twigs

Bud Type: ○ Terminal (grows at tip of a shoot causing shoot to grow longer)
○ Lateral (grow along sides of a shoot causing sideways growth)

Twig Features: ○ Smooth ○ Hairy ○ Spines ○ Corky Ribs
○ (Other) _____

Notes: _____

Bark

Texture: ○ Furrowed ○ Scaly ○ Peeling ○ Smooth ○ Shiny
○ Fissured ○ Ridges / Depressions ○ Papery ○ Warty
○ (Other) _____

Color: ○ Gray ○ Brown ○ Cinnamon ○ White ○ Silver
○ Green ○ Copper ○ (Other) _____

Notes: _____

Ash

Sassafras

American Beech

Elm

Eastern White Pine

Tulip

Catalpa

Fir

Yellow Birch

Aspen

Maple

Sycamore

Spruce

Ash

Sassafras

American Beech

Elm

Eastern White Pine

Tulip

Catalpa

Fir

Yellow Birch

Aspen

Maple

Sycamore

Spruce

Environment

Location / GPS: _____ Date _____

Season: ○ Spring   ○ Summer   ○ Fall   ○ Winter

Surroundings: ○ Hedgerows   ○ Field   ○ Park   ○ Woodland   ○ Water
○ Other_____

Setting: ○ Natural   ○ Artificial   **Type:** ○ Evergreen   ○ Deciduous

Notes: _____
_____

General

Shape: ○ Vase   ○ Columnar   ○ Round   ○ (Other) _____

Features: ○ Conical/Spire   ○ Spreading   ○ Upright   ○ Weeping
○ (Other) _____

Branching: ○ Opposite   ○ Alternate   **Estimated Age:** _____

Notes: _____
_____

Needles or Leaves

Type: ○ Needle   ○ Simple Broadleaf   ○ Compound Broadleaf   ○ Scales

Shape: ○ Cordate (heart-shaped)   ○ Lanceolate (long and narrow)
○ Deltoid (triangular)   ○ Obicular (round)   ○ Ovate (egg-shaped)
○ Palm and Maple   ○ Lobed

Structure: ○ Simple (attached to twigs or twig stems)
○ Compound (attached to single lead steam)

Notes: _____
_____

Flowers, Fruits & Seeds

Flower Type: ○ Single Blooms   ○ Clustered Blooms   ○ Catkins

Fruits / Seeds: ○ Berries   ○ Apples   ○ Pears   ○ Nuts   ○ Acorns
○ Cones   ○ Capsules   ○ Catkins   ○ (Other) _____

Notes: _____
_____

Leaf Buds & Twigs

Bud Type: ○ Terminal (grows at tip of a shoot causing shoot to grow longer)
○ Lateral (grow along sides of a shoot causing sideways growth)

Twig Features: ○ Smooth   ○ Hairy   ○ Spines   ○ Corky Ribs
○ (Other) _____

Notes: _____

Bark

Texture: ○ Furrowed   ○ Scaly   ○ Peeling   ○ Smooth   ○ Shiny
○ Fissured   ○ Ridges / Depressions   ○ Papery   ○ Warty
○ (Other) _____

Color: ○ Gray   ○ Brown   ○ Cinnamon   ○ White   ○ Silver
○ Green   ○ Copper   ○ (Other) _____

Notes: _____

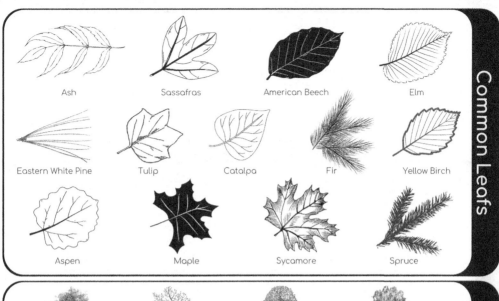

Ash Sassafras American Beech Elm

Eastern White Pine Tulip Catalpa Fir Yellow Birch

Aspen Maple Sycamore Spruce

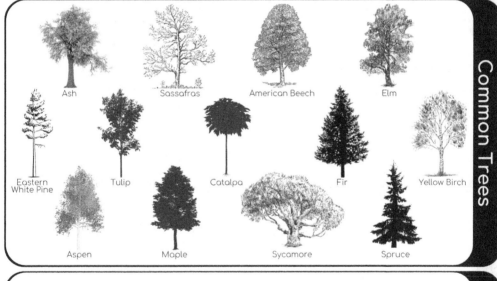

Ash Sassafras American Beech Elm

Eastern White Pine Tulip Catalpa Fir Yellow Birch

Aspen Maple Sycamore Spruce

Environment

Location / GPS: _____ Date _____

Season: ○ Spring ○ Summer ○ Fall ○ Winter

Surroundings: ○ Hedgerows ○ Field ○ Park ○ Woodland ○ Water
○ Other _____

Setting: ○ Natural ○ Artificial   Type: ○ Evergreen ○ Deciduous

Notes: _____
_____

General

Shape: ○ Vase ○ Columnar ○ Round ○ (Other) _____

Features: ○ Conical/Spire ○ Spreading ○ Upright ○ Weeping
○ (Other) _____

Branching: ○ Opposite ○ Alternate   Estimated Age: _____

Notes: _____
_____

Needles or Leaves

Type: ○ Needle ○ Simple Broadleaf ○ Compound Broadleaf ○ Scales

Shape: ○ Cordate (heart-shaped) ○ Lanceolate (long and narrow)
○ Deltoid (triangular) ○ Obicular (round) ○ Ovate (egg-shaped)
○ Palm and Maple ○ Lobed

Structure: ○ Simple (attached to twigs or twig stems)
○ Compound (attached to single lead steam)

Notes: _____
_____

Flowers, Fruits & Seeds

Flower Type: ○ Single Blooms ○ Clustered Blooms ○ Catkins

Fruits / Seeds: ○ Berries ○ Apples ○ Pears ○ Nuts ○ Acorns
○ Cones ○ Capsules ○ Catkins ○ (Other) _____

Notes: _____
_____

Leaf Buds & Twigs

Bud Type: ○ Terminal (grows at tip of a shoot causing shoot to grow longer)
○ Lateral (grow along sides of a shoot causing sideways growth)

Twig Features: ○ Smooth ○ Hairy ○ Spines ○ Corky Ribs
○ (Other) _____

Notes: _____

Bark

Texture: ○ Furrowed ○ Scaly ○ Peeling ○ Smooth ○ Shiny
○ Fissured ○ Ridges / Depressions ○ Papery ○ Warty
○ (Other) _____

Color: ○ Gray ○ Brown ○ Cinnamon ○ White ○ Silver
○ Green ○ Copper ○ (Other) _____

Notes: _____

Ash

Sassafras

American Beech

Elm

Eastern White Pine

Tulip

Catalpa

Fir

Yellow Birch

Aspen

Maple

Sycamore

Spruce

Ash

Sassafras

American Beech

Elm

Eastern White Pine

Tulip

Catalpa

Fir

Yellow Birch

Aspen

Maple

Sycamore

Spruce

Environment

Location / GPS: _____ Date _____

Season: ◯ Spring ◯ Summer ◯ Fall ◯ Winter

Surroundings: ◯ Hedgerows ◯ Field ◯ Park ◯ Woodland ◯ Water
◯ Other_____

Setting: ◯ Natural ◯ Artificial **Type:** ◯ Evergreen ◯ Deciduous

Notes: _____
_____

General

Shape: ◯ Vase ◯ Columnar ◯ Round ◯ (Other) _____

Features: ◯ Conical/Spire ◯ Spreading ◯ Upright ◯ Weeping
◯ (Other) _____

Branching: ◯ Opposite ◯ Alternate **Estimated Age:** _____

Notes: _____
_____

Needles or Leaves

Type: ◯ Needle ◯ Simple Broadleaf ◯ Compound Broadleaf ◯ Scales

Shape: ◯ Cordate (heart-shaped) ◯ Lanceolate (long and narrow)
◯ Deltoid (triangular) ◯ Obicular (round) ◯ Ovate (egg-shaped)
◯ Palm and Maple ◯ Lobed

Structure: ◯ Simple (attached to twigs or twig stems)
◯ Compound (attached to single lead steam)

Notes: _____
_____

Flowers, Fruits & Seeds

Flower Type: ◯ Single Blooms ◯ Clustered Blooms ◯ Catkins

Fruits / Seeds: ◯ Berries ◯ Apples ◯ Pears ◯ Nuts ◯ Acorns
◯ Cones ◯ Capsules ◯ Catkins ◯ (Other) _____

Notes: _____
_____

Leaf Buds & Twigs

Bud Type: ◯ Terminal (grows at tip of a shoot causing shoot to grow longer)
◯ Lateral (grow along sides of a shoot causing sideways growth)

Twig Features: ◯ Smooth ◯ Hairy ◯ Spines ◯ Corky Ribs
◯ (Other) _____

Notes: _____

Bark

Texture: ◯ Furrowed ◯ Scaly ◯ Peeling ◯ Smooth ◯ Shiny
◯ Fissured ◯ Ridges / Depressions ◯ Papery ◯ Warty
◯ (Other) _____

Color: ◯ Gray ◯ Brown ◯ Cinnamon ◯ White ◯ Silver
◯ Green ◯ Copper ◯ (Other) _____

Notes: _____

Ash

Sassafras

American Beech

Elm

Eastern White Pine

Tulip

Catalpa

Fir

Yellow Birch

Aspen

Maple

Sycamore

Spruce

Ash

Sassafras

American Beech

Elm

Eastern White Pine

Tulip

Catalpa

Fir

Yellow Birch

Aspen

Maple

Sycamore

Spruce

Environment

Location / GPS: _____ Date _____

Season: ○ Spring ○ Summer ○ Fall ○ Winter

Surroundings: ○ Hedgerows ○ Field ○ Park ○ Woodland ○ Water
○ Other _____

Setting: ○ Natural ○ Artificial   Type: ○ Evergreen ○ Deciduous

Notes: _____
_____

General

Shape: ○ Vase ○ Columnar ○ Round ○ (Other) _____

Features: ○ Conical/Spire ○ Spreading ○ Upright ○ Weeping
○ (Other) _____

Branching: ○ Opposite ○ Alternate   Estimated Age: _____

Notes: _____
_____

Needles or Leaves

Type: ○ Needle ○ Simple Broadleaf ○ Compound Broadleaf ○ Scales

Shape: ○ Cordate (heart-shaped) ○ Lanceolate (long and narrow)
○ Deltoid (triangular) ○ Obicular (round) ○ Ovate (egg-shaped)
○ Palm and Maple ○ Lobed

Structure: ○ Simple (attached to twigs or twig stems)
○ Compound (attached to single lead steam)

Notes: _____
_____

Flowers, Fruits & Seeds

Flower Type: ○ Single Blooms ○ Clustered Blooms ○ Catkins

Fruits / Seeds: ○ Berries ○ Apples ○ Pears ○ Nuts ○ Acorns
○ Cones ○ Capsules ○ Catkins ○ (Other) _____

Notes: _____
_____

Leaf Buds & Twigs

Bud Type: ○ Terminal (grows at tip of a shoot causing shoot to grow longer)
○ Lateral (grow along sides of a shoot causing sideways growth)

Twig Features: ○ Smooth ○ Hairy ○ Spines ○ Corky Ribs
○ (Other) _____

Notes: _____

Bark

Texture: ○ Furrowed ○ Scaly ○ Peeling ○ Smooth ○ Shiny
○ Fissured ○ Ridges / Depressions ○ Papery ○ Warty
○ (Other) _____

Color: ○ Gray ○ Brown ○ Cinnamon ○ White ○ Silver
○ Green ○ Copper ○ (Other) _____

Notes: _____

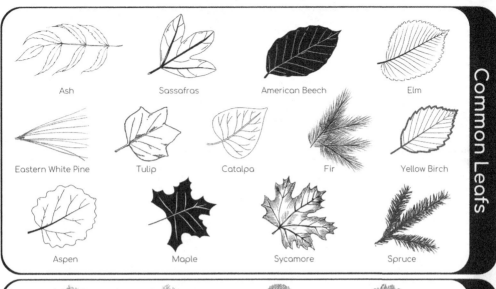

Ash · Sassafras · American Beech · Elm
Eastern White Pine · Tulip · Catalpa · Fir · Yellow Birch
Aspen · Maple · Sycamore · Spruce

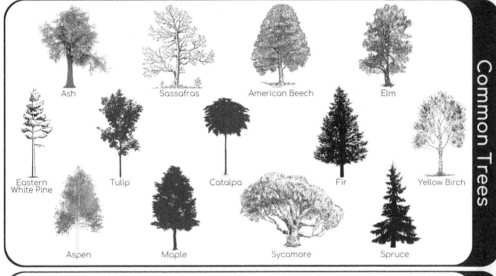

Ash · Sassafras · American Beech · Elm
Eastern White Pine · Tulip · Catalpa · Fir · Yellow Birch
Aspen · Maple · Sycamore · Spruce

Environment

Location / GPS: _____ Date _____

Season: ○ Spring ○ Summer ○ Fall ○ Winter

Surroundings: ○ Hedgerows ○ Field ○ Park ○ Woodland ○ Water
○ Other_____

Setting: ○ Natural ○ Artificial **Type:** ○ Evergreen ○ Deciduous

Notes: _____
_____

General

Shape: ○ Vase ○ Columnar ○ Round ○ (Other) _____

Features: ○ Conical/Spire ○ Spreading ○ Upright ○ Weeping
○ (Other) _____

Branching: ○ Opposite ○ Alternate **Estimated Age:** _____

Notes: _____
_____

Needles or Leaves

Type: ○ Needle ○ Simple Broadleaf ○ Compound Broadleaf ○ Scales

Shape: ○ Cordate (heart-shaped) ○ Lanceolate (long and narrow)
○ Deltoid (triangular) ○ Obicular (round) ○ Ovate (egg-shaped)
○ Palm and Maple ○ Lobed

Structure: ○ Simple (attached to twigs or twig stems)
○ Compound (attached to single lead steam)

Notes: _____
_____

Flowers, Fruits & Seeds

Flower Type: ○ Single Blooms ○ Clustered Blooms ○ Catkins

Fruits / Seeds: ○ Berries ○ Apples ○ Pears ○ Nuts ○ Acorns
○ Cones ○ Capsules ○ Catkins ○ (Other) _____

Notes: _____
_____

Leaf Buds & Twigs

Bud Type: ○ Terminal (grows at tip of a shoot causing shoot to grow longer)
○ Lateral (grow along sides of a shoot causing sideways growth)

Twig Features: ○ Smooth ○ Hairy ○ Spines ○ Corky Ribs
○ (Other) _____

Notes: _____

Bark

Texture: ○ Furrowed ○ Scaly ○ Peeling ○ Smooth ○ Shiny
○ Fissured ○ Ridges / Depressions ○ Papery ○ Warty
○ (Other) _____

Color: ○ Gray ○ Brown ○ Cinnamon ○ White ○ Silver
○ Green ○ Copper ○ (Other) _____

Notes: _____

Ash

Sassafras

American Beech

Elm

Eastern White Pine

Tulip

Catalpa

Fir

Yellow Birch

Aspen

Maple

Sycamore

Spruce

Ash

Sassafras

American Beech

Elm

Eastern White Pine

Tulip

Catalpa

Fir

Yellow Birch

Aspen

Maple

Sycamore

Spruce

Environment

Location / GPS: _____ Date _____

Season: ○ Spring ○ Summer ○ Fall ○ Winter

Surroundings: ○ Hedgerows ○ Field ○ Park ○ Woodland ○ Water
○ Other_____

Setting: ○ Natural ○ Artificial   Type: ○ Evergreen ○ Deciduous

Notes: _____
_____

General

Shape: ○ Vase ○ Columnar ○ Round ○ (Other) _____

Features: ○ Conical/Spire ○ Spreading ○ Upright ○ Weeping
○ (Other) _____

Branching: ○ Opposite ○ Alternate   Estimated Age: _____

Notes: _____
_____

Needles or Leaves

Type: ○ Needle ○ Simple Broadleaf ○ Compound Broadleaf ○ Scales

Shape: ○ Cordate (heart-shaped) ○ Lanceolate (long and narrow)
○ Deltoid (triangular) ○ Obicular (round) ○ Ovate (egg-shaped)
○ Palm and Maple ○ Lobed

Structure: ○ Simple (attached to twigs or twig stems)
○ Compound (attached to single lead steam)

Notes: _____
_____

Flowers, Fruits & Seeds

Flower Type: ○ Single Blooms ○ Clustered Blooms ○ Catkins

Fruits / Seeds: ○ Berries ○ Apples ○ Pears ○ Nuts ○ Acorns
○ Cones ○ Capsules ○ Catkins ○ (Other) _____

Notes: _____
_____

Leaf Buds & Twigs

Bud Type: ○ Terminal (grows at tip of a shoot causing shoot to grow longer)
○ Lateral (grow along sides of a shoot causing sideways growth)

Twig Features: ○ Smooth ○ Hairy ○ Spines ○ Corky Ribs
○ (Other) _____

Notes: _____

Bark

Texture: ○ Furrowed ○ Scaly ○ Peeling ○ Smooth ○ Shiny
○ Fissured ○ Ridges / Depressions ○ Papery ○ Warty
○ (Other) _____

Color: ○ Gray ○ Brown ○ Cinnamon ○ White ○ Silver
○ Green ○ Copper ○ (Other) _____

Notes: _____

Ash

Sassafras

American Beech

Elm

Eastern White Pine

Tulip

Catalpa

Fir

Yellow Birch

Aspen

Maple

Sycamore

Spruce

Ash

Sassafras

American Beech

Elm

Eastern White Pine

Tulip

Catalpa

Fir

Yellow Birch

Aspen

Maple

Sycamore

Spruce

Environment

Location / GPS: _____ Date _____

Season: ○ Spring ○ Summer ○ Fall ○ Winter

Surroundings: ○ Hedgerows ○ Field ○ Park ○ Woodland ○ Water
○ Other _____

Setting: ○ Natural ○ Artificial **Type:** ○ Evergreen ○ Deciduous

Notes: _____
_____

General

Shape: ○ Vase ○ Columnar ○ Round ○ (Other) _____

Features: ○ Conical/Spire ○ Spreading ○ Upright ○ Weeping
○ (Other) _____

Branching: ○ Opposite ○ Alternate **Estimated Age:** _____

Notes: _____
_____

Needles or Leaves

Type: ○ Needle ○ Simple Broadleaf ○ Compound Broadleaf ○ Scales

Shape: ○ Cordate (heart-shaped) ○ Lanceolate (long and narrow)
○ Deltoid (triangular) ○ Obicular (round) ○ Ovate (egg-shaped)
○ Palm and Maple ○ Lobed

Structure: ○ Simple (attached to twigs or twig stems)
○ Compound (attached to single lead steam)

Notes: _____
_____

Flowers, Fruits & Seeds

Flower Type: ○ Single Blooms ○ Clustered Blooms ○ Catkins

Fruits / Seeds: ○ Berries ○ Apples ○ Pears ○ Nuts ○ Acorns
○ Cones ○ Capsules ○ Catkins ○ (Other) _____

Notes: _____
_____

Leaf Buds & Twigs

Bud Type: ○ Terminal (grows at tip of a shoot causing shoot to grow longer)
○ Lateral (grow along sides of a shoot causing sideways growth)

Twig Features: ○ Smooth ○ Hairy ○ Spines ○ Corky Ribs
○ (Other) _____

Notes: _____

Bark

Texture: ○ Furrowed ○ Scaly ○ Peeling ○ Smooth ○ Shiny
○ Fissured ○ Ridges / Depressions ○ Papery ○ Warty
○ (Other) _____

Color: ○ Gray ○ Brown ○ Cinnamon ○ White ○ Silver
○ Green ○ Copper ○ (Other) _____

Notes: _____

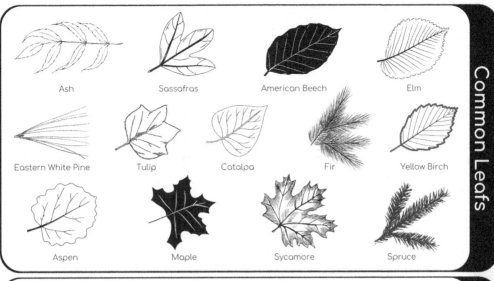

Ash Sassafras American Beech Elm

Eastern White Pine Tulip Catalpa Fir Yellow Birch

Aspen Maple Sycamore Spruce

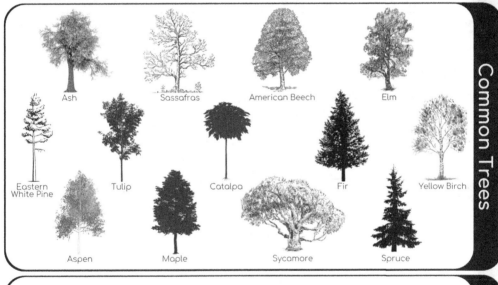

Ash Sassafras American Beech Elm

Eastern White Pine Tulip Catalpa Fir Yellow Birch

Aspen Maple Sycamore Spruce

Environment

Location / GPS: _____ Date _____

Season: ◯ Spring ◯ Summer ◯ Fall ◯ Winter

Surroundings: ◯ Hedgerows ◯ Field ◯ Park ◯ Woodland ◯ Water
◯ Other_____

Setting: ◯ Natural ◯ Artificial **Type:** ◯ Evergreen ◯ Deciduous

Notes: _____
_____

General

Shape: ◯ Vase ◯ Columnar ◯ Round ◯(Other) _____

Features: ◯ Conical/Spire ◯ Spreading ◯ Upright ◯ Weeping
◯(Other) _____

Branching: ◯ Opposite ◯ Alternate **Estimated Age:** _____

Notes: _____
_____

Needles or Leaves

Type: ◯ Needle ◯ Simple Broadleaf ◯ Compound Broadleaf ◯ Scales

Shape: ◯ Cordate (heart-shaped) ◯ Lanceolate (long and narrow)
◯ Deltoid (triangular) ◯ Obicular (round) ◯ Ovate (egg-shaped)
◯ Palm and Maple ◯ Lobed

Structure: ◯ Simple (attached to twigs or twig stems)
◯ Compound (attached to single lead steam)

Notes: _____
_____

Flowers, Fruits & Seeds

Flower Type: ◯ Single Blooms ◯ Clustered Blooms ◯ Catkins

Fruits / Seeds: ◯ Berries ◯ Apples ◯ Pears ◯ Nuts ◯ Acorns
◯ Cones ◯ Capsules ◯ Catkins ◯(Other) _____

Notes: _____
_____

Leaf Buds & Twigs

Bud Type: ◯ Terminal (grows at tip of a shoot causing shoot to grow longer)
◯ Lateral (grow along sides of a shoot causing sideways growth)

Twig Features: ◯ Smooth ◯ Hairy ◯ Spines ◯ Corky Ribs
◯(Other) _____

Notes: _____

Bark

Texture: ◯ Furrowed ◯ Scaly ◯ Peeling ◯ Smooth ◯ Shiny
◯ Fissured ◯ Ridges / Depressions ◯ Papery ◯ Warty
◯(Other) _____

Color: ◯ Gray ◯ Brown ◯ Cinnamon ◯ White ◯ Silver
◯ Green ◯ Copper ◯(Other) _____

Notes: _____

Ash

Sassafras

American Beech

Elm

Eastern White Pine

Tulip

Catalpa

Fir

Yellow Birch

Aspen

Maple

Sycamore

Spruce

Ash

Sassafras

American Beech

Elm

Eastern White Pine

Tulip

Catalpa

Fir

Yellow Birch

Aspen

Maple

Sycamore

Spruce

Environment

Location / GPS: _____ Date _____

Season: ○ Spring ○ Summer ○ Fall ○ Winter

Surroundings: ○ Hedgerows ○ Field ○ Park ○ Woodland ○ Water
○ Other_____

Setting: ○ Natural ○ Artificial   **Type:** ○ Evergreen ○ Deciduous

Notes: _____
_____

General

Shape: ○ Vase ○ Columnar ○ Round ○ (Other) _____

Features: ○ Conical/Spire ○ Spreading ○ Upright ○ Weeping
○ (Other) _____

Branching: ○ Opposite ○ Alternate   **Estimated Age:** _____

Notes: _____
_____

Needles or Leaves

Type: ○ Needle ○ Simple Broadleaf ○ Compound Broadleaf ○ Scales

Shape: ○ Cordate (heart-shaped) ○ Lanceolate (long and narrow)
○ Deltoid (triangular) ○ Obicular (round) ○ Ovate (egg-shaped)
○ Palm and Maple ○ Lobed

Structure: ○ Simple (attached to twigs or twig stems)
○ Compound (attached to single lead steam)

Notes: _____
_____

Flowers, Fruits & Seeds

Flower Type: ○ Single Blooms ○ Clustered Blooms ○ Catkins

Fruits / Seeds: ○ Berries ○ Apples ○ Pears ○ Nuts ○ Acorns
○ Cones ○ Capsules ○ Catkins ○ (Other) _____

Notes: _____
_____

Leaf Buds & Twigs

Bud Type: ○ Terminal (grows at tip of a shoot causing shoot to grow longer)
○ Lateral (grow along sides of a shoot causing sideways growth)

Twig Features: ○ Smooth ○ Hairy ○ Spines ○ Corky Ribs
○ (Other) _____

Notes: _____

Bark

Texture: ○ Furrowed ○ Scaly ○ Peeling ○ Smooth ○ Shiny
○ Fissured ○ Ridges / Depressions ○ Papery ○ Warty
○ (Other) _____

Color: ○ Gray ○ Brown ○ Cinnamon ○ White ○ Silver
○ Green ○ Copper ○ (Other) _____

Notes: _____

Ash

Sassafras

American Beech

Elm

Eastern White Pine

Tulip

Catalpa

Fir

Yellow Birch

Aspen

Maple

Sycamore

Spruce

Ash

Sassafras

American Beech

Elm

Eastern White Pine

Tulip

Catalpa

Fir

Yellow Birch

Aspen

Maple

Sycamore

Spruce

Environment

Location / GPS: _____ Date _____

Season: ◯ Spring ◯ Summer ◯ Fall ◯ Winter

Surroundings: ◯ Hedgerows ◯ Field ◯ Park ◯ Woodland ◯ Water
◯ Other _____

Setting: ◯ Natural ◯ Artificial   Type: ◯ Evergreen ◯ Deciduous

Notes: _____
_____

General

Shape: ◯ Vase ◯ Columnar ◯ Round ◯ (Other) _____

Features: ◯ Conical/Spire ◯ Spreading ◯ Upright ◯ Weeping
◯ (Other) _____

Branching: ◯ Opposite ◯ Alternate   Estimated Age: _____

Notes: _____
_____

Needles or Leaves

Type: ◯ Needle ◯ Simple Broadleaf ◯ Compound Broadleaf ◯ Scales

Shape: ◯ Cordate (heart-shaped) ◯ Lanceolate (long and narrow)
◯ Deltoid (triangular) ◯ Obicular (round) ◯ Ovate (egg-shaped)
◯ Palm and Maple ◯ Lobed

Structure: ◯ Simple (attached to twigs or twig stems)
◯ Compound (attached to single lead steam)

Notes: _____
_____

Flowers, Fruits & Seeds

Flower Type: ◯ Single Blooms ◯ Clustered Blooms ◯ Catkins

Fruits / Seeds: ◯ Berries ◯ Apples ◯ Pears ◯ Nuts ◯ Acorns
◯ Cones ◯ Capsules ◯ Catkins ◯ (Other) _____

Notes: _____
_____

Leaf Buds & Twigs

Bud Type: ◯ Terminal (grows at tip of a shoot causing shoot to grow longer)
◯ Lateral (grow along sides of a shoot causing sideways growth)

Twig Features: ◯ Smooth ◯ Hairy ◯ Spines ◯ Corky Ribs
◯ (Other) _____

Notes: _____

Bark

Texture: ◯ Furrowed ◯ Scaly ◯ Peeling ◯ Smooth ◯ Shiny
◯ Fissured ◯ Ridges / Depressions ◯ Papery ◯ Warty
◯ (Other) _____

Color: ◯ Gray ◯ Brown ◯ Cinnamon ◯ White ◯ Silver
◯ Green ◯ Copper ◯ (Other) _____

Notes: _____

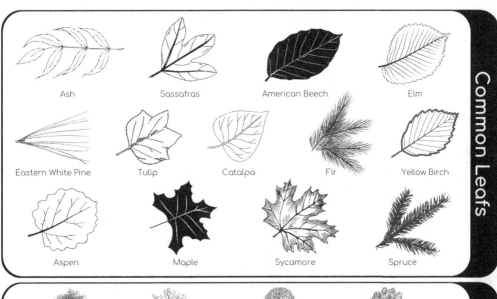

Ash · Sassafras · American Beech · Elm · Eastern White Pine · Tulip · Catalpa · Fir · Yellow Birch · Aspen · Maple · Sycamore · Spruce

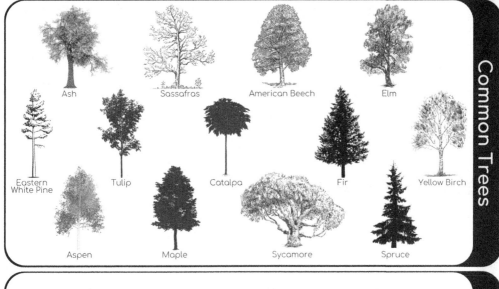

Ash · Sassafras · American Beech · Elm · Eastern White Pine · Tulip · Catalpa · Fir · Yellow Birch · Aspen · Maple · Sycamore · Spruce

Environment

Location / GPS: _____ Date _____

Season: ◯ Spring ◯ Summer ◯ Fall ◯ Winter

Surroundings: ◯ Hedgerows ◯ Field ◯ Park ◯ Woodland ◯ Water
◯ Other _____

Setting: ◯ Natural ◯ Artificial **Type:** ◯ Evergreen ◯ Deciduous

Notes: _____
_____

General

Shape: ◯ Vase ◯ Columnar ◯ Round ◯ (Other) _____

Features: ◯ Conical/Spire ◯ Spreading ◯ Upright ◯ Weeping
◯ (Other) _____

Branching: ◯ Opposite ◯ Alternate **Estimated Age:** _____

Notes: _____
_____

Needles or Leaves

Type: ◯ Needle ◯ Simple Broadleaf ◯ Compound Broadleaf ◯ Scales

Shape: ◯ Cordate (heart-shaped) ◯ Lanceolate (long and narrow)
◯ Deltoid (triangular) ◯ Obicular (round) ◯ Ovate (egg-shaped)
◯ Palm and Maple ◯ Lobed

Structure: ◯ Simple (attached to twigs or twig stems)
◯ Compound (attached to single lead steam)

Notes: _____
_____

Flowers, Fruits & Seeds

Flower Type: ◯ Single Blooms ◯ Clustered Blooms ◯ Catkins

Fruits / Seeds: ◯ Berries ◯ Apples ◯ Pears ◯ Nuts ◯ Acorns
◯ Cones ◯ Capsules ◯ Catkins ◯ (Other) _____

Notes: _____
_____

Leaf Buds & Twigs

Bud Type: ◯ Terminal (grows at tip of a shoot causing shoot to grow longer)
◯ Lateral (grow along sides of a shoot causing sideways growth)

Twig Features: ◯ Smooth ◯ Hairy ◯ Spines ◯ Corky Ribs
◯ (Other) _____

Notes: _____

Bark

Texture: ◯ Furrowed ◯ Scaly ◯ Peeling ◯ Smooth ◯ Shiny
◯ Fissured ◯ Ridges / Depressions ◯ Papery ◯ Warty
◯ (Other) _____

Color: ◯ Gray ◯ Brown ◯ Cinnamon ◯ White ◯ Silver
◯ Green ◯ Copper ◯ (Other) _____

Notes: _____

Ash

Sassafras

American Beech

Elm

Eastern White Pine

Tulip

Catalpa

Fir

Yellow Birch

Aspen

Maple

Sycamore

Spruce

Ash

Sassafras

American Beech

Elm

Eastern White Pine

Tulip

Catalpa

Fir

Yellow Birch

Aspen

Maple

Sycamore

Spruce

Environment

Location / GPS: _____ Date _____

Season: ◯ Spring ◯ Summer ◯ Fall ◯ Winter

Surroundings: ◯ Hedgerows ◯ Field ◯ Park ◯ Woodland ◯ Water
◯ Other _____

Setting: ◯ Natural ◯ Artificial **Type:** ◯ Evergreen ◯ Deciduous

Notes: _____
_____

General

Shape: ◯ Vase ◯ Columnar ◯ Round ◯ (Other) _____

Features: ◯ Conical/Spire ◯ Spreading ◯ Upright ◯ Weeping
◯ (Other) _____

Branching: ◯ Opposite ◯ Alternate **Estimated Age:** _____

Notes: _____
_____

Needles or Leaves

Type: ◯ Needle ◯ Simple Broadleaf ◯ Compound Broadleaf ◯ Scales

Shape: ◯ Cordate (heart-shaped) ◯ Lanceolate (long and narrow)
◯ Deltoid (triangular) ◯ Obicular (round) ◯ Ovate (egg-shaped)
◯ Palm and Maple ◯ Lobed

Structure: ◯ Simple (attached to twigs or twig stems)
◯ Compound (attached to single lead steam)

Notes: _____
_____

Flowers, Fruits & Seeds

Flower Type: ◯ Single Blooms ◯ Clustered Blooms ◯ Catkins

Fruits / Seeds: ◯ Berries ◯ Apples ◯ Pears ◯ Nuts ◯ Acorns
◯ Cones ◯ Capsules ◯ Catkins ◯ (Other) _____

Notes: _____
_____

Leaf Buds & Twigs

Bud Type: ◯ Terminal (grows at tip of a shoot causing shoot to grow longer)
◯ Lateral (grow along sides of a shoot causing sideways growth)

Twig Features: ◯ Smooth ◯ Hairy ◯ Spines ◯ Corky Ribs
◯ (Other) _____

Notes: _____

Bark

Texture: ◯ Furrowed ◯ Scaly ◯ Peeling ◯ Smooth ◯ Shiny
◯ Fissured ◯ Ridges / Depressions ◯ Papery ◯ Warty
◯ (Other) _____

Color: ◯ Gray ◯ Brown ◯ Cinnamon ◯ White ◯ Silver
◯ Green ◯ Copper ◯ (Other) _____

Notes: _____

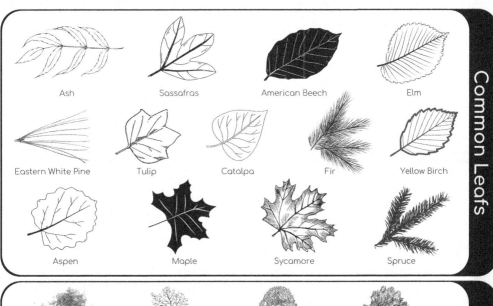

Ash — Sassafras — American Beech — Elm

Eastern White Pine — Tulip — Catalpa — Fir — Yellow Birch

Aspen — Maple — Sycamore — Spruce

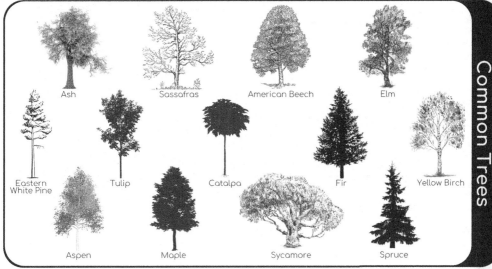

Ash — Sassafras — American Beech — Elm

Eastern White Pine — Tulip — Catalpa — Fir — Yellow Birch

Aspen — Maple — Sycamore — Spruce

Environment

Location / GPS: _____ Date _____

Season: ○ Spring ○ Summer ○ Fall ○ Winter

Surroundings: ○ Hedgerows ○ Field ○ Park ○ Woodland ○ Water
○ Other _____

Setting: ○ Natural ○ Artificial **Type:** ○ Evergreen ○ Deciduous

Notes: _____
_____

General

Shape: ○ Vase ○ Columnar ○ Round ○ (Other) _____

Features: ○ Conical/Spire ○ Spreading ○ Upright ○ Weeping
○ (Other) _____

Branching: ○ Opposite ○ Alternate **Estimated Age:** _____

Notes: _____
_____

Needles or Leaves

Type: ○ Needle ○ Simple Broadleaf ○ Compound Broadleaf ○ Scales

Shape: ○ Cordate (heart-shaped) ○ Lanceolate (long and narrow)
○ Deltoid (triangular) ○ Obicular (round) ○ Ovate (egg-shaped)
○ Palm and Maple ○ Lobed

Structure: ○ Simple (attached to twigs or twig stems)
○ Compound (attached to single lead steam)

Notes: _____
_____

Flowers, Fruits & Seeds

Flower Type: ○ Single Blooms ○ Clustered Blooms ○ Catkins

Fruits / Seeds: ○ Berries ○ Apples ○ Pears ○ Nuts ○ Acorns
○ Cones ○ Capsules ○ Catkins ○ (Other) _____

Notes: _____
_____

Leaf Buds & Twigs

Bud Type: ○ Terminal (grows at tip of a shoot causing shoot to grow longer)
○ Lateral (grow along sides of a shoot causing sideways growth)

Twig Features: ○ Smooth ○ Hairy ○ Spines ○ Corky Ribs
○ (Other) _____

Notes: _____

Bark

Texture: ○ Furrowed ○ Scaly ○ Peeling ○ Smooth ○ Shiny
○ Fissured ○ Ridges / Depressions ○ Papery ○ Warty
○ (Other) _____

Color: ○ Gray ○ Brown ○ Cinnamon ○ White ○ Silver
○ Green ○ Copper ○ (Other) _____

Notes: _____

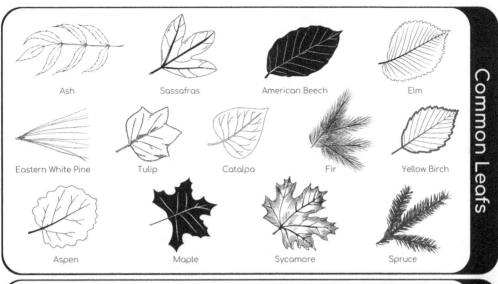

Ash · Sassafras · American Beech · Elm · Eastern White Pine · Tulip · Catalpa · Fir · Yellow Birch · Aspen · Maple · Sycamore · Spruce

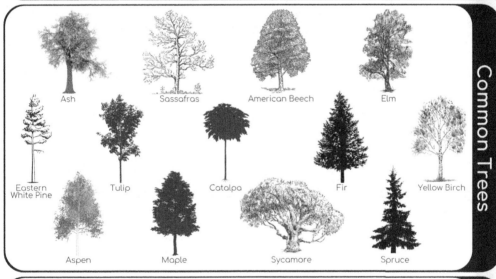

Ash · Sassafras · American Beech · Elm · Eastern White Pine · Tulip · Catalpa · Fir · Yellow Birch · Aspen · Maple · Sycamore · Spruce

Environment

Location / GPS: _____ Date _____

Season: ○ Spring ○ Summer ○ Fall ○ Winter

Surroundings: ○ Hedgerows ○ Field ○ Park ○ Woodland ○ Water
○ Other _____

Setting: ○ Natural ○ Artificial   Type: ○ Evergreen ○ Deciduous

Notes: _____
_____

General

Shape: ○ Vase ○ Columnar ○ Round ○ (Other) _____

Features: ○ Conical/Spire ○ Spreading ○ Upright ○ Weeping
○ (Other) _____

Branching: ○ Opposite ○ Alternate   Estimated Age: _____

Notes: _____
_____

Needles or Leaves

Type: ○ Needle ○ Simple Broadleaf ○ Compound Broadleaf ○ Scales

Shape: ○ Cordate (heart-shaped) ○ Lanceolate (long and narrow)
○ Deltoid (triangular) ○ Obicular (round) ○ Ovate (egg-shaped)
○ Palm and Maple ○ Lobed

Structure: ○ Simple (attached to twigs or twig stems)
○ Compound (attached to single lead steam)

Notes: _____
_____

Flowers, Fruits & Seeds

Flower Type: ○ Single Blooms ○ Clustered Blooms ○ Catkins

Fruits / Seeds: ○ Berries ○ Apples ○ Pears ○ Nuts ○ Acorns
○ Cones ○ Capsules ○ Catkins ○ (Other) _____

Notes: _____
_____

Leaf Buds & Twigs

Bud Type: ○ Terminal (grows at tip of a shoot causing shoot to grow longer)
○ Lateral (grow along sides of a shoot causing sideways growth)

Twig Features: ○ Smooth ○ Hairy ○ Spines ○ Corky Ribs
○ (Other) _____

Notes: _____

Bark

Texture: ○ Furrowed ○ Scaly ○ Peeling ○ Smooth ○ Shiny
○ Fissured ○ Ridges / Depressions ○ Papery ○ Warty
○ (Other) _____

Color: ○ Gray ○ Brown ○ Cinnamon ○ White ○ Silver
○ Green ○ Copper ○ (Other) _____

Notes: _____

Ash

Sassafras

American Beech

Elm

Eastern White Pine

Tulip

Catalpa

Fir

Yellow Birch

Aspen

Maple

Sycamore

Spruce

Ash

Sassafras

American Beech

Elm

Eastern White Pine

Tulip

Catalpa

Fir

Yellow Birch

Aspen

Maple

Sycamore

Spruce

Environment

Location / GPS: _____ Date _____

Season: ◯ Spring ◯ Summer ◯ Fall ◯ Winter

Surroundings: ◯ Hedgerows ◯ Field ◯ Park ◯ Woodland ◯ Water
◯ Other _____

Setting: ◯ Natural ◯ Artificial **Type:** ◯ Evergreen ◯ Deciduous

Notes: _____
_____

General

Shape: ◯ Vase ◯ Columnar ◯ Round ◯ (Other) _____

Features: ◯ Conical/Spire ◯ Spreading ◯ Upright ◯ Weeping
◯ (Other) _____

Branching: ◯ Opposite ◯ Alternate **Estimated Age:** _____

Notes: _____
_____

Needles or Leaves

Type: ◯ Needle ◯ Simple Broadleaf ◯ Compound Broadleaf ◯ Scales

Shape: ◯ Cordate (heart-shaped) ◯ Lanceolate (long and narrow)
◯ Deltoid (triangular) ◯ Obicular (round) ◯ Ovate (egg-shaped)
◯ Palm and Maple ◯ Lobed

Structure: ◯ Simple (attached to twigs or twig stems)
◯ Compound (attached to single lead steam)

Notes: _____
_____

Flowers, Fruits & Seeds

Flower Type: ◯ Single Blooms ◯ Clustered Blooms ◯ Catkins

Fruits / Seeds: ◯ Berries ◯ Apples ◯ Pears ◯ Nuts ◯ Acorns
◯ Cones ◯ Capsules ◯ Catkins ◯ (Other) _____

Notes: _____
_____

Leaf Buds & Twigs

Bud Type: ◯ Terminal (grows at tip of a shoot causing shoot to grow longer)
◯ Lateral (grow along sides of a shoot causing sideways growth)

Twig Features: ◯ Smooth ◯ Hairy ◯ Spines ◯ Corky Ribs
◯ (Other) _____

Notes: _____

Bark

Texture: ◯ Furrowed ◯ Scaly ◯ Peeling ◯ Smooth ◯ Shiny
◯ Fissured ◯ Ridges / Depressions ◯ Papery ◯ Warty
◯ (Other) _____

Color: ◯ Gray ◯ Brown ◯ Cinnamon ◯ White ◯ Silver
◯ Green ◯ Copper ◯ (Other) _____

Notes: _____

Ash

Sassafras

American Beech

Elm

Eastern White Pine

Tulip

Catalpa

Fir

Yellow Birch

Aspen

Maple

Sycamore

Spruce

Ash

Sassafras

American Beech

Elm

Eastern White Pine

Tulip

Catalpa

Fir

Yellow Birch

Aspen

Maple

Sycamore

Spruce

Environment

Location / GPS: _____ Date _____

Season: ○ Spring ○ Summer ○ Fall ○ Winter

Surroundings: ○ Hedgerows ○ Field ○ Park ○ Woodland ○ Water
○ Other _____

Setting: ○ Natural ○ Artificial **Type:** ○ Evergreen ○ Deciduous

Notes: _____
_____

General

Shape: ○ Vase ○ Columnar ○ Round ○ (Other) _____

Features: ○ Conical/Spire ○ Spreading ○ Upright ○ Weeping
○ (Other) _____

Branching: ○ Opposite ○ Alternate **Estimated Age:** _____

Notes: _____
_____

Needles or Leaves

Type: ○ Needle ○ Simple Broadleaf ○ Compound Broadleaf ○ Scales

Shape: ○ Cordate (heart-shaped) ○ Lanceolate (long and narrow)
○ Deltoid (triangular) ○ Obicular (round) ○ Ovate (egg-shaped)
○ Palm and Maple ○ Lobed

Structure: ○ Simple (attached to twigs or twig stems)
○ Compound (attached to single lead steam)

Notes: _____
_____

Flowers, Fruits & Seeds

Flower Type: ○ Single Blooms ○ Clustered Blooms ○ Catkins

Fruits / Seeds: ○ Berries ○ Apples ○ Pears ○ Nuts ○ Acorns
○ Cones ○ Capsules ○ Catkins ○ (Other) _____

Notes: _____
_____

Leaf Buds & Twigs

Bud Type: ○ Terminal (grows at tip of a shoot causing shoot to grow longer)
○ Lateral (grow along sides of a shoot causing sideways growth)

Twig Features: ○ Smooth ○ Hairy ○ Spines ○ Corky Ribs
○ (Other) _____

Notes: _____

Bark

Texture: ○ Furrowed ○ Scaly ○ Peeling ○ Smooth ○ Shiny
○ Fissured ○ Ridges / Depressions ○ Papery ○ Warty
○ (Other) _____

Color: ○ Gray ○ Brown ○ Cinnamon ○ White ○ Silver
○ Green ○ Copper ○ (Other) _____

Notes: _____

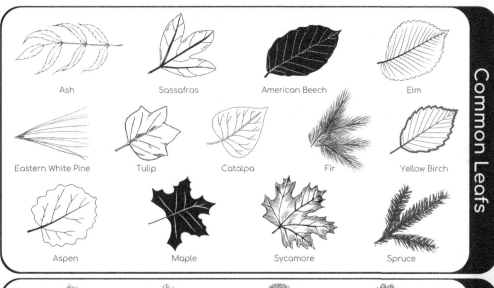

Ash · Sassafras · American Beech · Elm · Eastern White Pine · Tulip · Catalpa · Fir · Yellow Birch · Aspen · Maple · Sycamore · Spruce

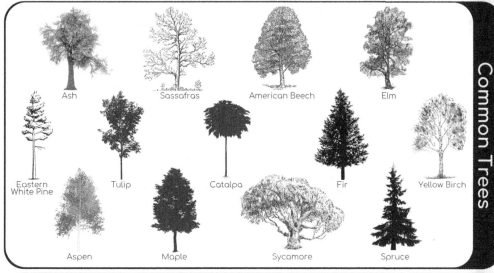

Ash · Sassafras · American Beech · Elm · Eastern White Pine · Tulip · Catalpa · Fir · Yellow Birch · Aspen · Maple · Sycamore · Spruce

_____
_____
_____
_____
_____
_____
_____
_____
_____
_____
_____

Environment

Location / GPS: _____ Date _____

Season: ○ Spring ○ Summer ○ Fall ○ Winter

Surroundings: ○ Hedgerows ○ Field ○ Park ○ Woodland ○ Water
○ Other _____

Setting: ○ Natural ○ Artificial **Type:** ○ Evergreen ○ Deciduous

Notes: _____
_____

General

Shape: ○ Vase ○ Columnar ○ Round ○ (Other) _____

Features: ○ Conical/Spire ○ Spreading ○ Upright ○ Weeping
○ (Other) _____

Branching: ○ Opposite ○ Alternate **Estimated Age:** _____

Notes: _____
_____

Needles or Leaves

Type: ○ Needle ○ Simple Broadleaf ○ Compound Broadleaf ○ Scales

Shape: ○ Cordate (heart-shaped) ○ Lanceolate (long and narrow)
○ Deltoid (triangular) ○ Obicular (round) ○ Ovate (egg-shaped)
○ Palm and Maple ○ Lobed

Structure: ○ Simple (attached to twigs or twig stems)
○ Compound (attached to single lead steam)

Notes: _____
_____

Flowers, Fruits & Seeds

Flower Type: ○ Single Blooms ○ Clustered Blooms ○ Catkins

Fruits / Seeds: ○ Berries ○ Apples ○ Pears ○ Nuts ○ Acorns
○ Cones ○ Capsules ○ Catkins ○ (Other) _____

Notes: _____
_____

Leaf Buds & Twigs

Bud Type: ○ Terminal (grows at tip of a shoot causing shoot to grow longer)
○ Lateral (grow along sides of a shoot causing sideways growth)

Twig Features: ○ Smooth ○ Hairy ○ Spines ○ Corky Ribs
○ (Other) _____

Notes: _____

Bark

Texture: ○ Furrowed ○ Scaly ○ Peeling ○ Smooth ○ Shiny
○ Fissured ○ Ridges / Depressions ○ Papery ○ Warty
○ (Other) _____

Color: ○ Gray ○ Brown ○ Cinnamon ○ White ○ Silver
○ Green ○ Copper ○ (Other) _____

Notes: _____

Ash

Sassafras

American Beech

Elm

Eastern White Pine

Tulip

Catalpa

Fir

Yellow Birch

Aspen

Maple

Sycamore

Spruce

Ash

Sassafras

American Beech

Elm

Eastern White Pine

Tulip

Catalpa

Fir

Yellow Birch

Aspen

Maple

Sycamore

Spruce

Environment

Location / GPS: _____ Date _____

Season: ◯ Spring ◯ Summer ◯ Fall ◯ Winter

Surroundings: ◯ Hedgerows ◯ Field ◯ Park ◯ Woodland ◯ Water
◯ Other_____

Setting: ◯ Natural ◯ Artificial **Type:** ◯ Evergreen ◯ Deciduous

Notes:_____
_____

General

Shape: ◯ Vase ◯ Columnar ◯ Round ◯ (Other) _____

Features: ◯ Conical/Spire ◯ Spreading ◯ Upright ◯ Weeping
◯ (Other) _____

Branching: ◯ Opposite ◯ Alternate **Estimated Age:** _____

Notes: _____
_____

Needles or Leaves

Type: ◯ Needle ◯ Simple Broadleaf ◯ Compound Broadleaf ◯ Scales

Shape: ◯ Cordate (heart-shaped) ◯ Lanceolate (long and narrow)
◯ Deltoid (triangular) ◯ Obicular (round) ◯ Ovate (egg-shaped)
◯ Palm and Maple ◯ Lobed

Structure: ◯ Simple (attached to twigs or twig stems)
◯ Compound (attached to single lead steam)

Notes: _____
_____

Flowers, Fruits & Seeds

Flower Type: ◯ Single Blooms ◯ Clustered Blooms ◯ Catkins

Fruits / Seeds: ◯ Berries ◯ Apples ◯ Pears ◯ Nuts ◯ Acorns
◯ Cones ◯ Capsules ◯ Catkins ◯ (Other) _____

Notes: _____
_____

Leaf Buds & Twigs

Bud Type: ◯ Terminal (grows at tip of a shoot causing shoot to grow longer)
◯ Lateral (grow along sides of a shoot causing sideways growth)

Twig Features: ◯ Smooth ◯ Hairy ◯ Spines ◯ Corky Ribs
◯ (Other) _____

Notes: _____

Bark

Texture: ◯ Furrowed ◯ Scaly ◯ Peeling ◯ Smooth ◯ Shiny
◯ Fissured ◯ Ridges / Depressions ◯ Papery ◯ Warty
◯ (Other) _____

Color: ◯ Gray ◯ Brown ◯ Cinnamon ◯ White ◯ Silver
◯ Green ◯ Copper ◯ (Other) _____

Notes: _____

Ash

Sassafras

American Beech

Elm

Eastern White Pine

Tulip

Catalpa

Fir

Yellow Birch

Aspen

Maple

Sycamore

Spruce

Ash

Sassafras

American Beech

Elm

Eastern White Pine

Tulip

Catalpa

Fir

Yellow Birch

Aspen

Maple

Sycamore

Spruce

Environment

Location / GPS: _____ Date _____

Season: ○ Spring ○ Summer ○ Fall ○ Winter

Surroundings: ○ Hedgerows ○ Field ○ Park ○ Woodland ○ Water
○ Other_____

Setting: ○ Natural ○ Artificial **Type:** ○ Evergreen ○ Deciduous

Notes: _____
_____

General

Shape: ○ Vase ○ Columnar ○ Round ○ (Other) _____

Features: ○ Conical/Spire ○ Spreading ○ Upright ○ Weeping
○ (Other) _____

Branching: ○ Opposite ○ Alternate **Estimated Age:** _____

Notes: _____
_____

Needles or Leaves

Type: ○ Needle ○ Simple Broadleaf ○ Compound Broadleaf ○ Scales

Shape: ○ Cordate (heart-shaped) ○ Lanceolate (long and narrow)
○ Deltoid (triangular) ○ Obicular (round) ○ Ovate (egg-shaped)
○ Palm and Maple ○ Lobed

Structure: ○ Simple (attached to twigs or twig stems)
○ Compound (attached to single lead steam)

Notes: _____
_____

Flowers, Fruits & Seeds

Flower Type: ○ Single Blooms ○ Clustered Blooms ○ Catkins

Fruits / Seeds: ○ Berries ○ Apples ○ Pears ○ Nuts ○ Acorns
○ Cones ○ Capsules ○ Catkins ○ (Other) _____

Notes: _____
_____

Leaf Buds & Twigs

Bud Type: ○ Terminal (grows at tip of a shoot causing shoot to grow longer)
○ Lateral (grow along sides of a shoot causing sideways growth)

Twig Features: ○ Smooth ○ Hairy ○ Spines ○ Corky Ribs
○ (Other) _____

Notes: _____

Bark

Texture: ○ Furrowed ○ Scaly ○ Peeling ○ Smooth ○ Shiny
○ Fissured ○ Ridges / Depressions ○ Papery ○ Warty
○ (Other) _____

Color: ○ Gray ○ Brown ○ Cinnamon ○ White ○ Silver
○ Green ○ Copper ○ (Other) _____

Notes: _____

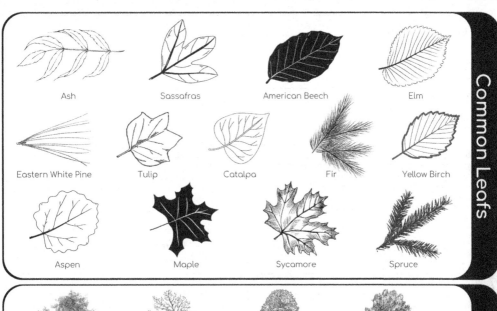

Ash · Sassafras · American Beech · Elm · Eastern White Pine · Tulip · Catalpa · Fir · Yellow Birch · Aspen · Maple · Sycamore · Spruce

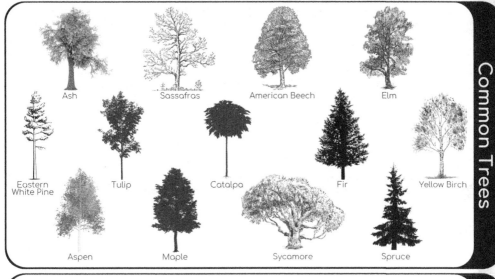

Ash · Sassafras · American Beech · Elm · Eastern White Pine · Tulip · Catalpa · Fir · Yellow Birch · Aspen · Maple · Sycamore · Spruce

Environment

Location / GPS: _____ Date _____

Season: ○ Spring ○ Summer ○ Fall ○ Winter

Surroundings: ○ Hedgerows ○ Field ○ Park ○ Woodland ○ Water
○ Other_____

Setting: ○ Natural ○ Artificial   Type: ○ Evergreen ○ Deciduous

Notes: _____
_____

General

Shape: ○ Vase ○ Columnar ○ Round ○ (Other) _____

Features: ○ Conical/Spire ○ Spreading ○ Upright ○ Weeping
○ (Other) _____

Branching: ○ Opposite ○ Alternate   Estimated Age: _____

Notes: _____
_____

Needles or Leaves

Type: ○ Needle ○ Simple Broadleaf ○ Compound Broadleaf ○ Scales

Shape: ○ Cordate (heart-shaped) ○ Lanceolate (long and narrow)
○ Deltoid (triangular) ○ Obicular (round) ○ Ovate (egg-shaped)
○ Palm and Maple ○ Lobed

Structure: ○ Simple (attached to twigs or twig stems)
○ Compound (attached to single lead steam)

Notes: _____
_____

Flowers, Fruits & Seeds

Flower Type: ○ Single Blooms ○ Clustered Blooms ○ Catkins

Fruits / Seeds: ○ Berries ○ Apples ○ Pears ○ Nuts ○ Acorns
○ Cones ○ Capsules ○ Catkins ○ (Other) _____

Notes: _____
_____

Leaf Buds & Twigs

Bud Type: ○ Terminal (grows at tip of a shoot causing shoot to grow longer)
○ Lateral (grow along sides of a shoot causing sideways growth)

Twig Features: ○ Smooth ○ Hairy ○ Spines ○ Corky Ribs
○ (Other) _____

Notes: _____

Bark

Texture: ○ Furrowed ○ Scaly ○ Peeling ○ Smooth ○ Shiny
○ Fissured ○ Ridges / Depressions ○ Papery ○ Warty
○ (Other) _____

Color: ○ Gray ○ Brown ○ Cinnamon ○ White ○ Silver
○ Green ○ Copper ○ (Other) _____

Notes: _____

Ash

Sassafras

American Beech

Elm

Eastern White Pine

Tulip

Catalpa

Fir

Yellow Birch

Aspen

Maple

Sycamore

Spruce

Ash

Sassafras

American Beech

Elm

Eastern White Pine

Tulip

Catalpa

Fir

Yellow Birch

Aspen

Maple

Sycamore

Spruce

Environment

Location / GPS: _____ Date _____

Season: ◯ Spring ◯ Summer ◯ Fall ◯ Winter

Surroundings: ◯ Hedgerows ◯ Field ◯ Park ◯ Woodland ◯ Water
◯ Other _____

Setting: ◯ Natural ◯ Artificial **Type:** ◯ Evergreen ◯ Deciduous

Notes: _____
_____

General

Shape: ◯ Vase ◯ Columnar ◯ Round ◯ (Other) _____

Features: ◯ Conical/Spire ◯ Spreading ◯ Upright ◯ Weeping
◯ (Other) _____

Branching: ◯ Opposite ◯ Alternate **Estimated Age:** _____

Notes: _____
_____

Needles or Leaves

Type: ◯ Needle ◯ Simple Broadleaf ◯ Compound Broadleaf ◯ Scales

Shape: ◯ Cordate (heart-shaped) ◯ Lanceolate (long and narrow)
◯ Deltoid (triangular) ◯ Obicular (round) ◯ Ovate (egg-shaped)
◯ Palm and Maple ◯ Lobed

Structure: ◯ Simple (attached to twigs or twig stems)
◯ Compound (attached to single lead steam)

Notes: _____
_____

Flowers, Fruits & Seeds

Flower Type: ◯ Single Blooms ◯ Clustered Blooms ◯ Catkins

Fruits / Seeds: ◯ Berries ◯ Apples ◯ Pears ◯ Nuts ◯ Acorns
◯ Cones ◯ Capsules ◯ Catkins ◯ (Other) _____

Notes: _____
_____

Leaf Buds & Twigs

Bud Type: ◯ Terminal (grows at tip of a shoot causing shoot to grow longer)
◯ Lateral (grow along sides of a shoot causing sideways growth)

Twig Features: ◯ Smooth ◯ Hairy ◯ Spines ◯ Corky Ribs
◯ (Other) _____

Notes: _____

Bark

Texture: ◯ Furrowed ◯ Scaly ◯ Peeling ◯ Smooth ◯ Shiny
◯ Fissured ◯ Ridges / Depressions ◯ Papery ◯ Warty
◯ (Other) _____

Color: ◯ Gray ◯ Brown ◯ Cinnamon ◯ White ◯ Silver
◯ Green ◯ Copper ◯ (Other) _____

Notes: _____

Ash

Sassafras

American Beech

Elm

Eastern White Pine

Tulip

Catalpa

Fir

Yellow Birch

Aspen

Maple

Sycamore

Spruce

Ash

Sassafras

American Beech

Elm

Eastern White Pine

Tulip

Catalpa

Fir

Yellow Birch

Aspen

Maple

Sycamore

Spruce

Environment

Location / GPS: _____ Date _____

Season: ⃝ Spring ⃝ Summer ⃝ Fall ⃝ Winter

Surroundings: ⃝ Hedgerows ⃝ Field ⃝ Park ⃝ Woodland ⃝ Water
⃝ Other_____

Setting: ⃝ Natural ⃝ Artificial **Type:** ⃝ Evergreen ⃝ Deciduous

Notes: _____
_____

General

Shape: ⃝ Vase ⃝ Columnar ⃝ Round ⃝ (Other) _____

Features: ⃝ Conical/Spire ⃝ Spreading ⃝ Upright ⃝ Weeping
⃝ (Other) _____

Branching: ⃝ Opposite ⃝ Alternate **Estimated Age:** _____

Notes: _____
_____

Needles or Leaves

Type: ⃝ Needle ⃝ Simple Broadleaf ⃝ Compound Broadleaf ⃝ Scales

Shape: ⃝ Cordate (heart-shaped) ⃝ Lanceolate (long and narrow)
⃝ Deltoid (triangular) ⃝ Obicular (round) ⃝ Ovate (egg-shaped)
⃝ Palm and Maple ⃝ Lobed

Structure: ⃝ Simple (attached to twigs or twig stems)
⃝ Compound (attached to single lead steam)

Notes: _____
_____

Flowers, Fruits & Seeds

Flower Type: ⃝ Single Blooms ⃝ Clustered Blooms ⃝ Catkins

Fruits / Seeds: ⃝ Berries ⃝ Apples ⃝ Pears ⃝ Nuts ⃝ Acorns
⃝ Cones ⃝ Capsules ⃝ Catkins ⃝ (Other) _____

Notes: _____
_____

Leaf Buds & Twigs

Bud Type: ⃝ Terminal (grows at tip of a shoot causing shoot to grow longer)
⃝ Lateral (grow along sides of a shoot causing sideways growth)

Twig Features: ⃝ Smooth ⃝ Hairy ⃝ Spines ⃝ Corky Ribs
⃝ (Other) _____

Notes: _____

Bark

Texture: ⃝ Furrowed ⃝ Scaly ⃝ Peeling ⃝ Smooth ⃝ Shiny
⃝ Fissured ⃝ Ridges / Depressions ⃝ Papery ⃝ Warty
⃝ (Other) _____

Color: ⃝ Gray ⃝ Brown ⃝ Cinnamon ⃝ White ⃝ Silver
⃝ Green ⃝ Copper ⃝ (Other) _____

Notes: _____

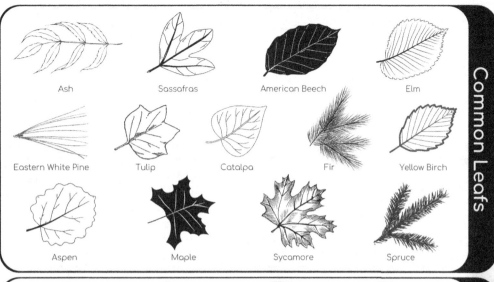

Ash

Sassafras

American Beech

Elm

Eastern White Pine

Tulip

Catalpa

Fir

Yellow Birch

Aspen

Maple

Sycamore

Spruce

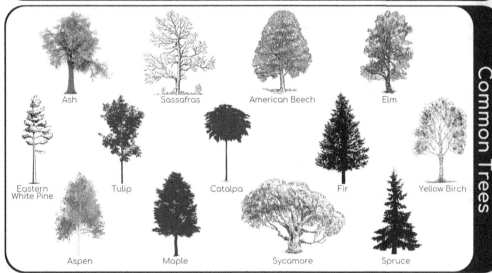

Ash

Sassafras

American Beech

Elm

Eastern White Pine

Tulip

Catalpa

Fir

Yellow Birch

Aspen

Maple

Sycamore

Spruce

Environment

Location / GPS: _____ Date _____

Season: ○ Spring   ○ Summer   ○ Fall   ○ Winter

Surroundings: ○ Hedgerows   ○ Field   ○ Park   ○ Woodland   ○ Water
○ Other_____

Setting: ○ Natural   ○ Artificial   Type: ○ Evergreen   ○ Deciduous

Notes: _____
_____

General

Shape: ○ Vase   ○ Columnar   ○ Round   ○ (Other) _____

Features: ○ Conical/Spire   ○ Spreading   ○ Upright   ○ Weeping
○ (Other) _____

Branching: ○ Opposite   ○ Alternate   Estimated Age: _____

Notes: _____
_____

Needles or Leaves

Type: ○ Needle   ○ Simple Broadleaf   ○ Compound Broadleaf   ○ Scales

Shape: ○ Cordate (heart-shaped)   ○ Lanceolate (long and narrow)
○ Deltoid (triangular)   ○ Obicular (round)   ○ Ovate (egg-shaped)
○ Palm and Maple   ○ Lobed

Structure: ○ Simple (attached to twigs or twig stems)
○ Compound (attached to single lead steam)

Notes: _____
_____

Flowers, Fruits & Seeds

Flower Type: ○ Single Blooms   ○ Clustered Blooms   ○ Catkins

Fruits / Seeds: ○ Berries   ○ Apples   ○ Pears   ○ Nuts   ○ Acorns
○ Cones   ○ Capsules   ○ Catkins   ○ (Other) _____

Notes: _____
_____

Leaf Buds & Twigs

Bud Type: ○ Terminal (grows at tip of a shoot causing shoot to grow longer)
○ Lateral (grow along sides of a shoot causing sideways growth)

Twig Features: ○ Smooth   ○ Hairy   ○ Spines   ○ Corky Ribs
○ (Other) _____

Notes: _____

Bark

Texture: ○ Furrowed   ○ Scaly   ○ Peeling   ○ Smooth   ○ Shiny
○ Fissured   ○ Ridges / Depressions   ○ Papery   ○ Warty
○ (Other) _____

Color: ○ Gray   ○ Brown   ○ Cinnamon   ○ White   ○ Silver
○ Green   ○ Copper   ○ (Other) _____

Notes: _____

Ash

Sassafras

American Beech

Elm

Eastern White Pine

Tulip

Catalpa

Fir

Yellow Birch

Aspen

Maple

Sycamore

Spruce

Ash

Sassafras

American Beech

Elm

Eastern White Pine

Tulip

Catalpa

Fir

Yellow Birch

Aspen

Maple

Sycamore

Spruce

Environment

Location / GPS: _____ Date _____

Season: ○ Spring ○ Summer ○ Fall ○ Winter

Surroundings: ○ Hedgerows ○ Field ○ Park ○ Woodland ○ Water
○ Other _____

Setting: ○ Natural ○ Artificial **Type:** ○ Evergreen ○ Deciduous

Notes: _____
_____

General

Shape: ○ Vase ○ Columnar ○ Round ○ (Other) _____

Features: ○ Conical/Spire ○ Spreading ○ Upright ○ Weeping
○ (Other) _____

Branching: ○ Opposite ○ Alternate **Estimated Age:** _____

Notes: _____
_____

Needles or Leaves

Type: ○ Needle ○ Simple Broadleaf ○ Compound Broadleaf ○ Scales

Shape: ○ Cordate (heart-shaped) ○ Lanceolate (long and narrow)
○ Deltoid (triangular) ○ Obicular (round) ○ Ovate (egg-shaped)
○ Palm and Maple ○ Lobed

Structure: ○ Simple (attached to twigs or twig stems)
○ Compound (attached to single lead steam)

Notes: _____
_____

Flowers, Fruits & Seeds

Flower Type: ○ Single Blooms ○ Clustered Blooms ○ Catkins

Fruits / Seeds: ○ Berries ○ Apples ○ Pears ○ Nuts ○ Acorns
○ Cones ○ Capsules ○ Catkins ○ (Other) _____

Notes: _____
_____

Leaf Buds & Twigs

Bud Type: ○ Terminal (grows at tip of a shoot causing shoot to grow longer)
○ Lateral (grow along sides of a shoot causing sideways growth)

Twig Features: ○ Smooth ○ Hairy ○ Spines ○ Corky Ribs
○ (Other) _____

Notes: _____

Bark

Texture: ○ Furrowed ○ Scaly ○ Peeling ○ Smooth ○ Shiny
○ Fissured ○ Ridges / Depressions ○ Papery ○ Warty
○ (Other) _____

Color: ○ Gray ○ Brown ○ Cinnamon ○ White ○ Silver
○ Green ○ Copper ○ (Other) _____

Notes: _____

Ash

Sassafras

American Beech

Elm

Eastern White Pine

Tulip

Catalpa

Fir

Yellow Birch

Aspen

Maple

Sycamore

Spruce

Ash

Sassafras

American Beech

Elm

Eastern White Pine

Tulip

Catalpa

Fir

Yellow Birch

Aspen

Maple

Sycamore

Spruce

Environment

Location / GPS: _____ Date _____

Season: ○ Spring ○ Summer ○ Fall ○ Winter

Surroundings: ○ Hedgerows ○ Field ○ Park ○ Woodland ○ Water
○ Other _____

Setting: ○ Natural ○ Artificial   **Type:** ○ Evergreen ○ Deciduous

Notes: _____
_____

General

Shape: ○ Vase ○ Columnar ○ Round ○ (Other) _____

Features: ○ Conical/Spire ○ Spreading ○ Upright ○ Weeping
○ (Other) _____

Branching: ○ Opposite ○ Alternate   Estimated Age: _____

Notes: _____
_____

Needles or Leaves

Type: ○ Needle ○ Simple Broadleaf ○ Compound Broadleaf ○ Scales

Shape: ○ Cordate (heart-shaped) ○ Lanceolate (long and narrow)
○ Deltoid (triangular) ○ Obicular (round) ○ Ovate (egg-shaped)
○ Palm and Maple ○ Lobed

Structure: ○ Simple (attached to twigs or twig stems)
○ Compound (attached to single lead steam)

Notes: _____
_____

Flowers, Fruits & Seeds

Flower Type: ○ Single Blooms ○ Clustered Blooms ○ Catkins

Fruits / Seeds: ○ Berries ○ Apples ○ Pears ○ Nuts ○ Acorns
○ Cones ○ Capsules ○ Catkins ○ (Other) _____

Notes: _____
_____

Leaf Buds & Twigs

Bud Type: ○ Terminal (grows at tip of a shoot causing shoot to grow longer)
○ Lateral (grow along sides of a shoot causing sideways growth)

Twig Features: ○ Smooth ○ Hairy ○ Spines ○ Corky Ribs
○ (Other) _____

Notes: _____

Bark

Texture: ○ Furrowed ○ Scaly ○ Peeling ○ Smooth ○ Shiny
○ Fissured ○ Ridges / Depressions ○ Papery ○ Warty
○ (Other) _____

Color: ○ Gray ○ Brown ○ Cinnamon ○ White ○ Silver
○ Green ○ Copper ○ (Other) _____

Notes: _____

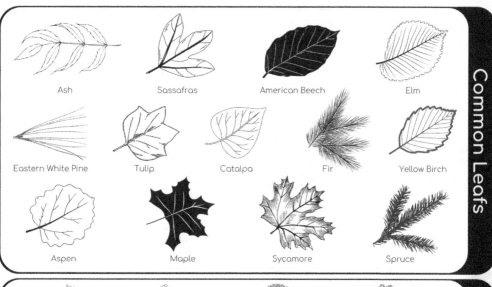

Ash

Sassafras

American Beech

Elm

Eastern White Pine

Tulip

Catalpa

Fir

Yellow Birch

Aspen

Maple

Sycamore

Spruce

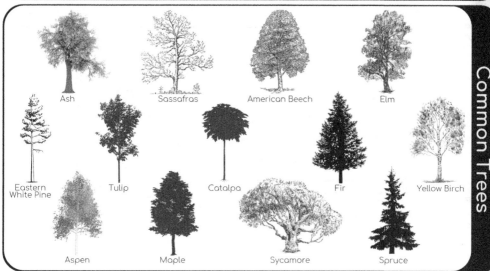

Ash

Sassafras

American Beech

Elm

Eastern White Pine

Tulip

Catalpa

Fir

Yellow Birch

Aspen

Maple

Sycamore

Spruce

Environment

Location / GPS: _____ Date _____

Season: ○ Spring ○ Summer ○ Fall ○ Winter

Surroundings: ○ Hedgerows ○ Field ○ Park ○ Woodland ○ Water
○ Other _____

Setting: ○ Natural ○ Artificial   Type: ○ Evergreen ○ Deciduous

Notes: _____
_____

General

Shape: ○ Vase ○ Columnar ○ Round ○ (Other) _____

Features: ○ Conical/Spire ○ Spreading ○ Upright ○ Weeping
○ (Other) _____

Branching: ○ Opposite ○ Alternate   Estimated Age: _____

Notes: _____
_____

Needles or Leaves

Type: ○ Needle ○ Simple Broadleaf ○ Compound Broadleaf ○ Scales

Shape: ○ Cordate (heart-shaped) ○ Lanceolate (long and narrow)
○ Deltoid (triangular) ○ Obicular (round) ○ Ovate (egg-shaped)
○ Palm and Maple ○ Lobed

Structure: ○ Simple (attached to twigs or twig stems)
○ Compound (attached to single lead steam)

Notes: _____
_____

Flowers, Fruits & Seeds

Flower Type: ○ Single Blooms ○ Clustered Blooms ○ Catkins

Fruits / Seeds: ○ Berries ○ Apples ○ Pears ○ Nuts ○ Acorns
○ Cones ○ Capsules ○ Catkins ○ (Other) _____

Notes: _____
_____

Leaf Buds & Twigs

Bud Type: ○ Terminal (grows at tip of a shoot causing shoot to grow longer)
○ Lateral (grow along sides of a shoot causing sideways growth)

Twig Features: ○ Smooth ○ Hairy ○ Spines ○ Corky Ribs
○ (Other) _____

Notes: _____

Bark

Texture: ○ Furrowed ○ Scaly ○ Peeling ○ Smooth ○ Shiny
○ Fissured ○ Ridges / Depressions ○ Papery ○ Warty
○ (Other) _____

Color: ○ Gray ○ Brown ○ Cinnamon ○ White ○ Silver
○ Green ○ Copper ○ (Other) _____

Notes: _____

Ash

Sassafras

American Beech

Elm

Eastern White Pine

Tulip

Catalpa

Fir

Yellow Birch

Aspen

Maple

Sycamore

Spruce

Common Trees

Ash

Sassafras

American Beech

Elm

Eastern White Pine

Tulip

Catalpa

Fir

Yellow Birch

Aspen

Maple

Sycamore

Spruce

Additional Notes

Environment

Location / GPS: _____ Date _____

Season: ○ Spring ○ Summer ○ Fall ○ Winter

Surroundings: ○ Hedgerows ○ Field ○ Park ○ Woodland ○ Water
 ○ Other _____

Setting: ○ Natural ○ Artificial **Type:** ○ Evergreen ○ Deciduous

Notes: _____
_____

General

Shape: ○ Vase ○ Columnar ○ Round ○ (Other) _____

Features: ○ Conical/Spire ○ Spreading ○ Upright ○ Weeping
 ○ (Other) _____

Branching: ○ Opposite ○ Alternate **Estimated Age:** _____

Notes: _____
_____

Needles or Leaves

Type: ○ Needle ○ Simple Broadleaf ○ Compound Broadleaf ○ Scales

Shape: ○ Cordate (heart-shaped) ○ Lanceolate (long and narrow)
 ○ Deltoid (triangular) ○ Obicular (round) ○ Ovate (egg-shaped)
 ○ Palm and Maple ○ Lobed

Structure: ○ Simple (attached to twigs or twig stems)
 ○ Compound (attached to single lead steam)

Notes: _____
_____

Flowers, Fruits & Seeds

Flower Type: ○ Single Blooms ○ Clustered Blooms ○ Catkins

Fruits / Seeds: ○ Berries ○ Apples ○ Pears ○ Nuts ○ Acorns
 ○ Cones ○ Capsules ○ Catkins ○ (Other) _____

Notes: _____
_____

Leaf Buds & Twigs

Bud Type: ○ Terminal (grows at tip of a shoot causing shoot to grow longer)
 ○ Lateral (grow along sides of a shoot causing sideways growth)

Twig Features: ○ Smooth ○ Hairy ○ Spines ○ Corky Ribs
 ○ (Other) _____

Notes: _____

Bark

Texture: ○ Furrowed ○ Scaly ○ Peeling ○ Smooth ○ Shiny
 ○ Fissured ○ Ridges / Depressions ○ Papery ○ Warty
 ○ (Other) _____

Color: ○ Gray ○ Brown ○ Cinnamon ○ White ○ Silver
 ○ Green ○ Copper ○ (Other) _____

Notes: _____

Ash

Sassafras

American Beech

Elm

Eastern White Pine

Tulip

Catalpa

Fir

Yellow Birch

Aspen

Maple

Sycamore

Spruce

Ash

Sassafras

American Beech

Elm

Eastern White Pine

Tulip

Catalpa

Fir

Yellow Birch

Aspen

Maple

Sycamore

Spruce

Environment

Location / GPS: _____ Date _____

Season: ○ Spring ○ Summer ○ Fall ○ Winter

Surroundings: ○ Hedgerows ○ Field ○ Park ○ Woodland ○ Water
○ Other _____

Setting: ○ Natural ○ Artificial **Type:** ○ Evergreen ○ Deciduous

Notes: _____
_____

General

Shape: ○ Vase ○ Columnar ○ Round ○ (Other) _____

Features: ○ Conical/Spire ○ Spreading ○ Upright ○ Weeping
○ (Other) _____

Branching: ○ Opposite ○ Alternate **Estimated Age:** _____

Notes: _____
_____

Needles or Leaves

Type: ○ Needle ○ Simple Broadleaf ○ Compound Broadleaf ○ Scales

Shape: ○ Cordate (heart-shaped) ○ Lanceolate (long and narrow)
○ Deltoid (triangular) ○ Obicular (round) ○ Ovate (egg-shaped)
○ Palm and Maple ○ Lobed

Structure: ○ Simple (attached to twigs or twig stems)
○ Compound (attached to single lead steam)

Notes: _____
_____

Flowers, Fruits & Seeds

Flower Type: ○ Single Blooms ○ Clustered Blooms ○ Catkins

Fruits / Seeds: ○ Berries ○ Apples ○ Pears ○ Nuts ○ Acorns
○ Cones ○ Capsules ○ Catkins ○ (Other) _____

Notes: _____
_____

Leaf Buds & Twigs

Bud Type: ○ Terminal (grows at tip of a shoot causing shoot to grow longer)
○ Lateral (grow along sides of a shoot causing sideways growth)

Twig Features: ○ Smooth ○ Hairy ○ Spines ○ Corky Ribs
○ (Other) _____

Notes: _____

Bark

Texture: ○ Furrowed ○ Scaly ○ Peeling ○ Smooth ○ Shiny
○ Fissured ○ Ridges / Depressions ○ Papery ○ Warty
○ (Other) _____

Color: ○ Gray ○ Brown ○ Cinnamon ○ White ○ Silver
○ Green ○ Copper ○ (Other) _____

Notes: _____

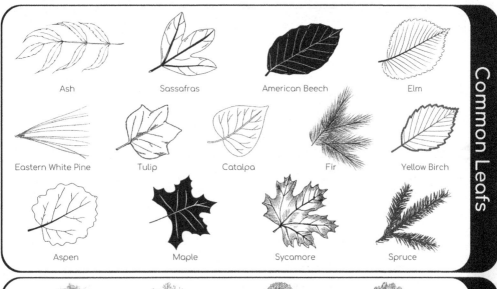

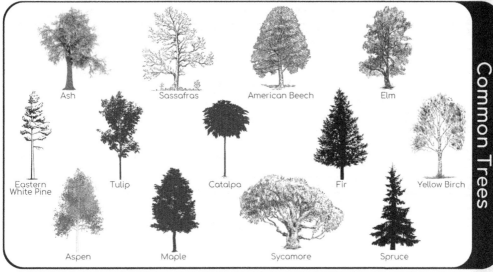

Environment

Location / GPS: _____ Date _____

Season: ⃝ Spring ⃝ Summer ⃝ Fall ⃝ Winter

Surroundings: ⃝ Hedgerows ⃝ Field ⃝ Park ⃝ Woodland ⃝ Water
⃝ Other_____

Setting: ⃝ Natural ⃝ Artificial   Type: ⃝ Evergreen ⃝ Deciduous

Notes: _____
_____

General

Shape: ⃝ Vase ⃝ Columnar ⃝ Round ⃝ (Other) _____

Features: ⃝ Conical/Spire ⃝ Spreading ⃝ Upright ⃝ Weeping
⃝ (Other) _____

Branching: ⃝ Opposite ⃝ Alternate   Estimated Age: _____

Notes: _____
_____

Needles or Leaves

Type: ⃝ Needle ⃝ Simple Broadleaf ⃝ Compound Broadleaf ⃝ Scales

Shape: ⃝ Cordate (heart-shaped) ⃝ Lanceolate (long and narrow)
⃝ Deltoid (triangular) ⃝ Obicular (round) ⃝ Ovate (egg-shaped)
⃝ Palm and Maple ⃝ Lobed

Structure: ⃝ Simple (attached to twigs or twig stems)
⃝ Compound (attached to single lead steam)

Notes: _____
_____

Flowers, Fruits & Seeds

Flower Type: ⃝ Single Blooms ⃝ Clustered Blooms ⃝ Catkins

Fruits / Seeds: ⃝ Berries ⃝ Apples ⃝ Pears ⃝ Nuts ⃝ Acorns
⃝ Cones ⃝ Capsules ⃝ Catkins ⃝ (Other) _____

Notes: _____
_____

Leaf Buds & Twigs

Bud Type: ⃝ Terminal (grows at tip of a shoot causing shoot to grow longer)
⃝ Lateral (grow along sides of a shoot causing sideways growth)

Twig Features: ⃝ Smooth ⃝ Hairy ⃝ Spines ⃝ Corky Ribs
⃝ (Other) _____

Notes: _____

Bark

Texture: ⃝ Furrowed ⃝ Scaly ⃝ Peeling ⃝ Smooth ⃝ Shiny
⃝ Fissured ⃝ Ridges / Depressions ⃝ Papery ⃝ Warty
⃝ (Other) _____

Color: ⃝ Gray ⃝ Brown ⃝ Cinnamon ⃝ White ⃝ Silver
⃝ Green ⃝ Copper ⃝ (Other) _____

Notes: _____

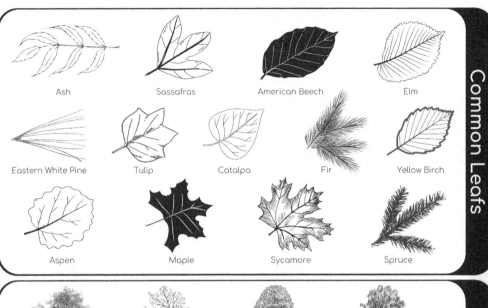

Ash
Sassafras
American Beech
Elm

Eastern White Pine
Tulip
Catalpa
Fir
Yellow Birch

Aspen
Maple
Sycamore
Spruce

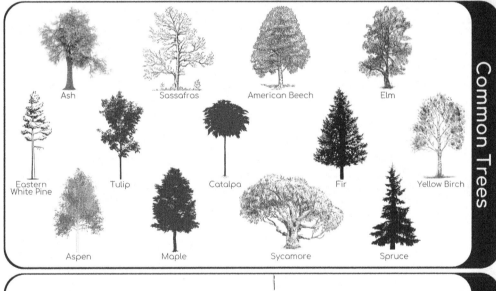

Ash
Sassafras
American Beech
Elm

Eastern White Pine
Tulip
Catalpa
Fir
Yellow Birch

Aspen
Maple
Sycamore
Spruce

Environment

Location / GPS: _____ Date _____

Season: ◯ Spring ◯ Summer ◯ Fall ◯ Winter

Surroundings: ◯ Hedgerows ◯ Field ◯ Park ◯ Woodland ◯ Water
◯ Other_____

Setting: ◯ Natural ◯ Artificial **Type:** ◯ Evergreen ◯ Deciduous

Notes: _____
_____

General

Shape: ◯ Vase ◯ Columnar ◯ Round ◯ (Other) _____

Features: ◯ Conical/Spire ◯ Spreading ◯ Upright ◯ Weeping
◯ (Other) _____

Branching: ◯ Opposite ◯ Alternate **Estimated Age:** _____

Notes: _____
_____

Needles or Leaves

Type: ◯ Needle ◯ Simple Broadleaf ◯ Compound Broadleaf ◯ Scales

Shape: ◯ Cordate (heart-shaped) ◯ Lanceolate (long and narrow)
◯ Deltoid (triangular) ◯ Obicular (round) ◯ Ovate (egg-shaped)
◯ Palm and Maple ◯ Lobed

Structure: ◯ Simple (attached to twigs or twig stems)
◯ Compound (attached to single lead steam)

Notes: _____
_____

Flowers, Fruits & Seeds

Flower Type: ◯ Single Blooms ◯ Clustered Blooms ◯ Catkins

Fruits / Seeds: ◯ Berries ◯ Apples ◯ Pears ◯ Nuts ◯ Acorns
◯ Cones ◯ Capsules ◯ Catkins ◯ (Other) _____

Notes: _____
_____

Leaf Buds & Twigs

Bud Type: ◯ Terminal (grows at tip of a shoot causing shoot to grow longer)
◯ Lateral (grow along sides of a shoot causing sideways growth)

Twig Features: ◯ Smooth ◯ Hairy ◯ Spines ◯ Corky Ribs
◯ (Other) _____

Notes: _____

Bark

Texture: ◯ Furrowed ◯ Scaly ◯ Peeling ◯ Smooth ◯ Shiny
◯ Fissured ◯ Ridges / Depressions ◯ Papery ◯ Warty
◯ (Other) _____

Color: ◯ Gray ◯ Brown ◯ Cinnamon ◯ White ◯ Silver
◯ Green ◯ Copper ◯ (Other) _____

Notes: _____

Ash

Sassafras

American Beech

Elm

Eastern White Pine

Tulip

Catalpa

Fir

Yellow Birch

Aspen

Maple

Sycamore

Spruce

Ash

Sassafras

American Beech

Elm

Eastern
White Pine

Tulip

Catalpa

Fir

Yellow Birch

Aspen

Maple

Sycamore

Spruce

Environment

Location / GPS: _____ Date _____

Season: ○ Spring ○ Summer ○ Fall ○ Winter

Surroundings: ○ Hedgerows ○ Field ○ Park ○ Woodland ○ Water
○ Other _____

Setting: ○ Natural ○ Artificial   Type: ○ Evergreen ○ Deciduous

Notes: _____
_____

General

Shape: ○ Vase ○ Columnar ○ Round ○ (Other) _____

Features: ○ Conical/Spire ○ Spreading ○ Upright ○ Weeping
○ (Other) _____

Branching: ○ Opposite ○ Alternate   Estimated Age: _____

Notes: _____
_____

Needles or Leaves

Type: ○ Needle ○ Simple Broadleaf ○ Compound Broadleaf ○ Scales

Shape: ○ Cordate (heart-shaped) ○ Lanceolate (long and narrow)
○ Deltoid (triangular) ○ Obicular (round) ○ Ovate (egg-shaped)
○ Palm and Maple ○ Lobed

Structure: ○ Simple (attached to twigs or twig stems)
○ Compound (attached to single lead steam)

Notes: _____
_____

Flowers, Fruits & Seeds

Flower Type: ○ Single Blooms ○ Clustered Blooms ○ Catkins

Fruits / Seeds: ○ Berries ○ Apples ○ Pears ○ Nuts ○ Acorns
○ Cones ○ Capsules ○ Catkins ○ (Other) _____

Notes: _____
_____

Leaf Buds & Twigs

Bud Type: ○ Terminal (grows at tip of a shoot causing shoot to grow longer)
○ Lateral (grow along sides of a shoot causing sideways growth)

Twig Features: ○ Smooth ○ Hairy ○ Spines ○ Corky Ribs
○ (Other) _____

Notes: _____

Bark

Texture: ○ Furrowed ○ Scaly ○ Peeling ○ Smooth ○ Shiny
○ Fissured ○ Ridges / Depressions ○ Papery ○ Warty
○ (Other) _____

Color: ○ Gray ○ Brown ○ Cinnamon ○ White ○ Silver
○ Green ○ Copper ○ (Other) _____

Notes: _____

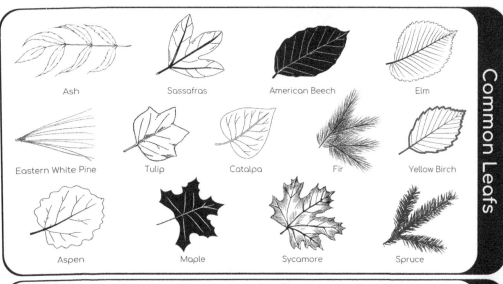

Ash

Sassafras

American Beech

Elm

Eastern White Pine

Tulip

Catalpa

Fir

Yellow Birch

Aspen

Maple

Sycamore

Spruce

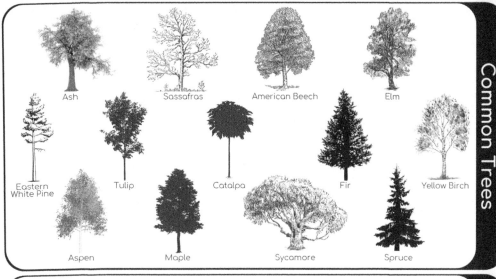

Ash

Sassafras

American Beech

Elm

Eastern White Pine

Tulip

Catalpa

Fir

Yellow Birch

Aspen

Maple

Sycamore

Spruce

Made in the USA
Monee, IL
16 July 2022

99810074R00066